Inside
Comprehensive Schools

by Tyrrell Burgess

London
Her Majesty's Stationery Office
1970

SBN 11 270149 3

Contents

Introduction

Schools are changing fast these days, and parents often feel bewildered by what goes on in them. Children are tackling new subjects and are being taught by new methods which seem very strange to their parents. The organization of schools is changing, too: the familiar landmark of the 11 plus is disappearing; "comprehensive" schools, "middle" schools and sixth form colleges are spreading. It is often hard to keep track of what is going on.

This book has been written to help parents and others to understand the schools, in particular the secondary schools. There is another book in this series, *Inside the Primary School* by John Blackie, which deals with education up to the age of 11 or so. Secondary education is for pupils over that age (though as we shall see there can be many variations in the age at which children change schools), and secondary education is changing faster than any other branch of education. So this book is also a guide to changes. It begins by showing why the 11 plus is being abolished, why we are "going comprehensive". It describes the way children transfer from one school to another and discusses a parent's right to choose a school. It then outlines the way children grow and develop—because today's educational methods are based upon this. But the bulk of the book is about the schools: what goes on inside them, how they are organized, what they hope to achieve. And because schools help to prepare their pupils for the adult world there is a chapter on the possibilities after school. A final chapter describes how a local education authority tackles the task of re-organizing its secondary schools "on comprehensive lines", and in the appendix you will find how far each authority has got with reorganization.

The book was commissioned by the Department of Education and Science—but it is a personal account of the schools and it expresses my own views. I have been particularly pleased to write it because, as I explain in Chapter One, I believe that the present reform of secondary education owes a great deal to parents. Comprehensive schools are their schools, and I hope this book will make clear what they have done.

Secondary education for all

What we are trying to do with all the present changes is to offer a full secondary education to all children. To understand what this means and why we are doing it only now, we have to look back a bit. During the second world war, as many people will remember, there was a great movement for social reform. People were determined that the country would not sink back into the miseries of the 1920s and 1930s. The most famous example was the campaign which surrounded the Beveridge Report, on which our whole system of social security is based. But there was a similar campaign for educational reform. Some say that it arose when the children who were evacuated from large cities were seen to have been reared in squalor and ignorance. Others point to the fact that the armed services discovered during the war people of high ability who had had little formal education. Whatever the reason, teachers and others were demanding reform during the early days of the war— and the old Board of Education responded by sending out its proposals in a document called the green book, because of the colour of its cover. The Board was flooded with replies, and there sprang up a Council for Educational Advance to agitate in earnest. The result was the Education Act, 1944, which is the basis of the modern education service. It is this Act which divided education into "three progressive stages"—primary, secondary and further—and its chief promise to the children of the nation was "secondary education for all." Before the war most children simply went through a single "elementary" school from the age of five to fourteen. A few were chosen for separate secondary schools at eleven or twelve.

What did "secondary" mean? Before 1944 there were regulations defining secondary education. They said that a secondary school was one for pupils intending to remain there for at least four years and to at least the age of 16. The school had to offer general education to an age range of at least 12 to 17, including instruction in mathematics, science and modern languages. But the most obvious mark of a secondary school was that its courses led to the School Leaving Certificate, certain credits in which were accepted as entry qualifications to the universities and the professions. This meant that secondary education was, in effect, the education of adolescents, offered subjects essential to life in the modern world and was a recognised route to further and higher education. It was this that should have been offered to all children after 1944. Unfortunately most of them still did not get it.

True, the Education Act, 1944, said that local education authorities had to provide enough schools offering secondary education, but this was defined as "full-time education suitable to the requirements of senior pupils"—and a senior pupil was simply "a person who has attained the age of 12 years but has not attained the age of 19 years"! These vague phrases did do some good: the requirement that the schools had to provide even for 18 year olds made it possible for large numbers of children to stay on at school beyond the compulsory school age. But they did mean that secondary education as previously understood was not provided for all after 1944. There was also the question of the school leaving age. Before 1944 it was 14. The Act provided for it to be raised to 16—because you cannot have secondary education without it. In 1947 it was in fact raised by one year, to 15, but for the final step we are having to wait until 1972— over a quarter of a century late.

At the same time the Ministry of Education made it clear that not all secondary schools could expect to be secondary in the old sense. There were to be "different types of secondary education": the former secondary schools became grammar schools, the former elementary schools became secondary moderns. The few secondary technical schools which had been founded remained as a third type in some areas. The Ministry said that the secondary modern schools would offer "a good all-round secondary education, not focused primarily on the traditional subjects of the school curriculum but developing out of the interests of the children". Up to a point, this can be seen as an early attempt to extend modern educational thinking into the secondary schools. We shall see more about this in Chapter Three. For the moment it is enough to say that the teachers in secondary modern schools did try to start with a new attitude to children and to the purposes of education. They distrusted the more arid aspects of the old academic curriculum. They saw, rightly, that there was a lot wrong with the traditional syllabuses and methods. Indeed they saw this more clearly than their colleagues in grammar schools. There was a very strong movement against limiting the curriculum by the demands of examinations. It would be wrong to imply that experiment was rife, but a number of secondary modern schools did develop new curricula, adopted new methods like projects and centres of interest, developed studies based on the children's own environment, introduced foreign languages and began creating new kinds of examinations which eventually culminated in the Certificate of Secondary Education.

But all this took time. The evolution of a new curriculum is never easy, and in the 1940s and 1950s teachers did not have the backing that now exists from bodies like the Schools Council and the Nuffield Foundation. Many of them were pioneering on their own. The spread of new ideas through the inspectorate was sure but slow. In many, perhaps most, secondary modern schools the curriculum remained basically the same as the old elementary school one and was secondary only in name. As late as 1961 an American visitor could describe these as "custodial" rather than educational institutions. This is not surprising. Educational change depends upon teachers, buildings and equipment, none of which were plentiful after the war. A really heroic effort was made to accommodate the extra year at school, called HORSA or the "hutted operation for raising the school age." And the Ministry of Education also did its best. All secondary schools were to have "parity of esteem"—and of accommodation and equipment. But the grammar schools had traditionally accommodated children beyond the school leaving age and offered an "academic" education. They were staffed and equipped to do so. They had three times as many graduates as secondary modern schools and had laboratories rather than craft rooms. It was clear that the educational opportunity offered in the two kinds of schools was markedly different.

Many cynical people said that what happened after the Education Act, 1944, was that the authorities simply made the best of a bad job. They took what schools there were and built an educational theory upon it. As there were different kinds of schools in each area, some method had to be found of deciding which children should go to which. And from this arose the whole apparatus of selection known as the 11 plus. In this the 11 year olds of an area were given tests which placed them in an order of ability. The available places in grammar schools were filled from the top of the list: the rest went to secondary moderns. But it is important to see that there were educational arguments for selection, arguments which many people still hold.

Selection rested upon three basic assumptions: first, that levels of ability stay roughly constant from the age of 11 onwards and that they can be accurately measured; second, that only a recognizable minority of children are capable of benefitting from an academic (or as I would say "secondary") education; and third, that the different abilities of children demand different schools—and in particular that the brighter children would be held back if they were educated with the rest. In recent years it has become clear that all these assumptions are false. There is no educational justification for selecting children for different kinds of schools at 11.

Let us look at these arguments a little more closely. Take the one about levels of ability. To be sure, the tests designed for the 11 plus are perhaps the best and fairest possible. They include verbal reasoning or intelligence tests and tests of achievement in English and arithmetic. Most local authorities also use teachers' recommendations, and some set essays and hold interviews. You can expect to find all these methods used where selection still takes place. Sometimes the tests are given on a single day, sometimes spread over a period. When the tests are marked, the children are placed in an order of merit.

To take intelligence tests as an example, their results give each child an "intelligence quotient" or IQ. This is the relation which a child's mental age bears to his chronological age. A child who does in the tests what the average ten year old can do has a mental age of ten. If a child is aged eight (and can do what the average ten year old can do) he has a mental age of ten and an IQ of $\frac{10}{8}$ x 100, which is 125. In other words an eight year old boy with an IQ of 125 will do as well in intelligence tests as the average boy of ten. You can work out other IQ examples for yourself. A boy of ten who does as well in an intelligence test as the average boy of eight is said to have an IQ of $\frac{8}{10}$ x 100, or 80. And so on.

All this sounds very precise. If you have a list of IQs and other test scores, can you not decide fairly who should go to which school? The answer is only very crudely at best, for a number of reasons. In the first place a child's performance can vary greatly from one test to the next, so a single test may produce an IQ which is widely wrong. Over a period of years the differences can be even greater, so that a decision based on a test taken at 11 may be wrong a year or two years later. The best we can say of an IQ of 95, for example, is that there is a ten to one chance that over the years it will be between 85 and 110. It is clear that drawing a line between children of similar IQs and sending some to grammar schools and some to secondary moderns is absurd and unjust. What is more, we are gradually coming to realise that although the tests seem to be educational, they are in effect social. The home backgrounds of children differ widely, and the children of manual workers or of poorly educated parents are likely to do less well in the normal intelligence test.

And of course, there are a whole lot of important qualities that the tests cannot measure. Intelligence is not the only thing needed for success at school, but it is the only thing that can be measured even as crudely as is now done. Other qualities, like conscientiousness, creativeness, judgment, industry, are not measured at all.

So we cannot yet measure the abilities of children precisely enough to make selection for different schools a sensible procedure—even though a lot of people in education thought for a long time that they could. But even if measurement were possible, to separate children into different kinds of schools would mean that we should have to be sure that their abilities did not change very much as they grew older. But this goes against everything that is known about children's growth and development. This is outlined more fully in Chapter Three, and parents who are interested should ask themselves as they read that chapter, how far it supports the idea of separate secondary schools. For the moment it is enough to mention one principle of development. A child's abilities are not the result of heredity alone, nor of environment alone, but of the interaction between the two. What you do to a child makes a difference. You can improve or impair his abilities. This is what education is all about. School is not just a place where children learn useful knowledge: it is a place where they develop their abilities. If a child's capacity is fixed at 11, why does he need to go to secondary school at all? The funny thing is that education actually works. This new view of ability was accepted officially by 1963, and it is not too much to say that selection was doomed at that point. In 1963, the Newsom Report was published and the then Minister of Education, Sir Edward Boyle, wrote in its foreword, "The essential point is that all children should have an equal opportunity *of acquiring intelligence* . . ." (my italics). If you think of schools as places where children acquire intelligence it is hard to use measures of intelligence to sort them out into different schools. It is not the business of teachers to accept a test score as final: it is their job to falsify the test, to help a child to achievements he never dreamed of. Any fool can make silk purses out of silk: it is the teacher's job to make them out of sows' ears.

The second assumption behind selection—that of a small minority capable of benefitting from grammar schools—was equally shaky. In one official report after another there were surveys showing that there were as many able children outside grammar schools as inside them. Large numbers of children, suitable even in terms of measured intelligence, were not being selected. And the old idea that for less intelligent children there should be a more limited curriculum was in very great doubt. There was even some evidence that such a curriculum in secondary modern schools was actually reducing the intelligence of the pupils over the four years of the course.

And of course the numbers going to grammar schools varied from one part of the country to another. In some places in Wales, 40 per cent of the children were selected for grammar schools, in some Lancashire boroughs only 15 per cent were selected. It seemed awfully far-fetched to believe that the minority capable of benefitting from grammar schools was 40 per cent in one place and 15 per cent in another. In fact the faith that this minority must be about 20 per cent overall stemmed from nothing more scientific than that about 20 per cent had had grammar school education in the past.

So we come to the last unwarranted assumption behind selection: that separate schools are needed for separate abilities. Of course children differ, and have different needs. The question is how these needs should be met. And it is fanciful to suppose that the wild diversity of children can somehow be matched by two (or at most three) types of secondary school. We need in fact the greatest variety of provision, and the argument should be about how to secure it. One particular worry should be dealt with at once. Will bright children be held back if they are not taught separately from the others? Most of the fears about this come from what people think happens in American high schools, which have always been comprehensive. But the traditions and practices of American education are so different from our own that the faults and virtues of their schools do not come only from their comprehensiveness. On the other hand, far more of the bright children "get on" and go further and higher education in America than in Britain. Experience in Britain does not suggest that in our comprehensives the more able suffer. When former grammar schools have been expanded into comprehensives they commonly found that more, not fewer, of their academic pupils stay on longer, get examination passes and go to university.

But perhaps the most remarkable evidence about this came not from Britain but from Sweden. In view of what I said about American experience, I ought to say at once that the Swedish system was very much like our own, in that it selected children for the equivalent of our grammar schools. In some ways their system was like ours before 1944! The Swedes suspected that selection was wrong, and arranged an experiment to decide. The city of Stockholm, the capital of Sweden and roughly the size of Liverpool, was divided into two. One half was reorganized along comprehensive lines and the other remained selective. The children in both halves were thoroughly tested at all stages of the change. What the Swedes discovered was that all groups of children, of all kinds of ability did either as well or better in the reorganized half than in the other—with one exception. This was a very small group of very bright working class boys. The significant thing was that this one setback was eliminated in two years, suggesting that it was the upheaval of change, not the new system, that had caused it. As a result of this experiment, the Swedish government decided to abolish selection. And all our experience in Britain suggests that if a similar experiment were conducted here the results would be very much the same. Our old arrangements, like those of Sweden, caused visible damage to the children of average and less than average intelligence, with no added advantages to the clever. The Swedes are also ahead in noting the weaknesses of their new system.

If the assumptions behind selection were wrong, its consequences in practice were no better. The tests at 11 distorted the curriculum of the primary schools, making teachers more reluctant to experiment or to introduce new subjects. However hard they tried to avoid it, "preparation" for the 11 plus was bound to dominate the last years of primary schools, and in some schools it became an obsession. The wisdom of "streaming" by ability was discussed less on its objective educational merits than on its supposed inevitability while the 11 plus lasted. So there was a good deal of pressure from primary school teachers against the whole business.

At the secondary stage, the difficulties faced by the secondary modern schools were unnecessarily daunting. A number of the schools rose above these difficulties, evolving new courses for the children whose ability was classed as "average" or "below average". Some of these courses were "unacademic" in the best sense. They related to the needs and interests of the pupils, but at the same time extended their capabilities in innumerable ways. A good deal of the success now being achieved in secondary schools of all kinds today is based upon the devotion and experience of secondary modern school teachers over the last twenty years or more. But again it would be wrong to paint too bright a picture. Dissatisfaction with the eleven plus did not arise from contentment with most secondary education. Whatever teachers and officials said, parents and pupils could not but feel that theirs were the schools for the "failures". The sense of rejection and demoralisation defeated many schools. The sentimental idea that the children who did not get to grammar school would be "good with their hands" was patronising and inaccurate. And those secondary moderns which managed, in spite of all, to build up academic sides and offer courses leading to the General Certificate of Education and other examinations merely called selection more urgently into question. There is no need to sneer at the secondary moderns: they did their task probably better than could have been expected and with a good deal of skill and devotion. It was the task they were given which was wrong: it arose from a failure of nerve and imagination and a shortage of men and materials after 1944.

The interesting thing is that parents realised all of this almost instinctively. Most parents would not have been able (reasonably enough) to say why the educational assumptions behind selection were wrong, but they did know how selection affected their children. And selection became unpopular with all those who had experience of it. Their dislike was founded on common sense and expressed in common sense terms. They saw, and resented, the differences in educational opportunity clearly offered in different types of schools. They regarded the attempt to assert that all schools had "parity of esteem" as sheer double-talk. All parents knew from simple observation that children develop at different rates and vary in their performance from day to day. So they knew that a test or even a series of tests taken at one time would be grossly unfair to late developers, and they guessed, even if they did not know the evidence, that the tests penalised the younger children in an age group and the children of poorer parents. The injustice of making a child's future depend upon his performance on a single day was so blatant that local authorities had quickly to spread the tests out over a period, but the sense of anger and frustration remained. Local authorities became extremely sensitive about their selection procedures. The National Foundation for Educational Research, which designed the tests, was prevented from saying publicly which authorities used which kinds of tests. The tests themselves were kept secret (with the one good motive of preventing "coaching") with the result that parents were even more worried and angry than they need have been and "pirate" tests had a field day. The upshot of all this was that by the middle 1950s parents as a whole had decided that selection was wrong. Without this public opinion selection would probably have survived. The volume of evidence against it from sociologists, psychologists and teachers was growing, but it might not have led to action unless it had chimed in with the public mood. The Labour and Liberal Parties were committed to ending selection from the late 1950s onwards, and by the middle 1960s the Conservative Party had come to realise that it was electoral folly to be labelled as defenders of the 11 plus. This has occurred because parents and others had made up their minds. The ending of selection is as nearly national policy as anything can be.

But ending selection was only half the argument. An equally important question is what should be put in its place. So far I have been talking almost entirely in terms of what was wrong with selection and of the arguments for abolishing it. And of course this is the way the argument went among parents and teachers, among sociologists and psychologists, at political meetings and so on. Parents may not know very much about detail and although they are quite capable of seeing when the results of a policy are dreadful, they may not know what policy would improve things. Fortunately there was a good deal of experience in comprehensive education in various parts of the country, so the alternative to a selective system was at hand. I have mentioned the arguments against selection: the whole of the rest of this book is in a sense the argument for comprehensives. It is perhaps enough to say briefly here that the positive benefits of comprehensive reorganization are that opportunities remain open for all children, up to the school leaving age; that the schools can offer a tremendous variety of courses; that teachers can be employed much more flexibly; and that all children share a common educational experience.

I have said that there was a good deal of experience in various parts of the country of comprehensive schools. Some people may wonder how this was possible. Broadly it is because the responsibility for schools rests with the local education authorities. These are the councils of counties, county boroughs, outer London boroughs and a committee of the Greater London Council called the Inner London Education Authority. It is they who must see that there are enough schools in their areas and who decide on the pattern of secondary education. The local education authorities are not entirely free: the Government controls, for example, the amount of educational building, so a local authority would not be able to build a school just to go comprehensive. It would have to justify it on increased numbers of children needing schools. Even so, a number of authorities, like London, Bristol and Coventry, had built a good number of comprehensive schools by the early 1960s. In some cases the authority was building such schools because it believed in them and thought selection should go. This is true of the authorities I have just mentioned. Others, like Devon, decided on comprehensives because it was the best way of providing secondary education in rural areas: they would otherwise have had to build very small secondary modern and grammar schools. Anglesey was fully comprehensive by 1953. Ironically, one authority, Westmorland, wanted to go comprehensive after the war but was prevented by the then Labour Government! So by the end of 1964, there were growing numbers of comprehensive schools in rural areas and on new housing estates.

The big change in policy, which started the reorganization of secondary education came in 1965. In January of that year, the House of Commons passed a motion which said:

"That this House, conscious of the need to raise educational standards at all levels, and regretting that the realisation of this objective is impeded by the separation of children into different types of secondary schools, notes with approval the efforts of local authorities to reorganize secondary education on comprehensive lines which will preserve all that is valuable in grammar school education for those children who now receive it and make it available to more children; recognises that the method and timing of such reorganization should vary to meet local needs; and believes that the time is now ripe for a declaration of national policy."

In July of the same year the Department of Education and Science sent out a circular to local authorities, Circular 10/65, saying that the Secretary of State "requests local education authorities, if they have not already done so, to prepare and submit to him plans for reorganizing secondary education in their areas on comprehensive lines" and giving some guidance on how to do it. You will notice that the

Secretary of State merely "requests": he had no power to compel local authorities, short of passing new laws. And the Department's circular offers "guidance": it does not tell local authorities what to do. What both the House of Commons motion and the Department's circular do is to recognise that reorganization is a local matter, and this is why parents will find that the ways local authorities are reorganizing vary substantially from one part of the country to another.

Circular 10/65 suggested six ways of going comprehensive which had so far emerged from experience and discussion. Most of them had already been in operation somewhere or other. The Circular recognised that although the needs of children were much the same anywhere the views of authorities, the distribution of population and the schools already existing would determine the precise way each authority chose. It was important, the circular said, "that new schemes build on the foundation of present achievements and preserve what is best in individual schools."

The six ways of going comprehensive were these:

(*a*) what the circular called the "orthodox" comprehensive school, taking all the secondary school children in a neighbourhood and offering them the full range of courses from 11 to 18.

(*b*) what was called a "two-tier" system, in which all the pupils went from primary school to a comprehensive school at 11 and then transferred from this school to another comprehensive school at 13 or 14.

(*c*) a scheme including "middle" schools. This became possible after the Education Act, 1964, allowed local authorities to vary the age of transfer from primary to secondary school from 11 plus. Under this system pupils are in primary schools until 8 or 9, in "middle" schools until 12 or 13 and in "upper" schools from there onwards. All these schools are of course comprehensive.

(*d*) schemes including sixth form colleges. In these pupils go to comprehensives schools from 11 to 16 (or perhaps 15) and those who are staying on into the sixth form do so in separate buildings. Sometimes the sixth form college is attached to one of the 11 to 16 schools.

All these four kinds of schemes were accepted by the circular as being acceptable long term ways of organizing secondary schools. Before mentioning the other two kinds of scheme, it is worth discussing these four a little more fully. The circular said that (a) would provide the simplest and best solution if we were starting a new pattern of secondary education from scratch, and it added that a six or seven form entry would be a reasonable size for a school of this type. (A "form-entry" means simply the number of children who would be taught as a class or form—say 30 children. A six form entry would therefore mean that six times 30, which is 180, children would enter the school in the first year. Such a school might have about 1,000 children in it altogether.).

The circular very much discouraged authorities from trying this kind of school where the buildings were not big enough and children had therefore to be split between a number of different buildings. Authorities which have put up such schemes have been urged to have two-tier ones instead.

The advantages of the all through school are that the educational experience of the children can be planned as a whole. If there is a new building it is not only much more pleasant but the building can also be designed from the school's educational principles. The Department and the local authorities are getting very good at this: school building is one of the greatest triumphs of the welfare state. Another advantage, on balance, is the size of these schools. Of course, there is a tradition of cosiness in education, of Mr. Chips' knowing every boy by name, but this seldom compensates for the limitations of small schools.

Large ones have to take care that pupils do not get neglected: all sorts of house or tutorial systems are described in chapter six. But a small school may be able to offer only one foreign language, a large one half a dozen. The range of accommodation and equipment in a large school can be very much greater. So can various kinds of teachers. Good graduate teachers who are attracted by sixth form work can also teach the younger and less able. Non-graduate teachers get the chance to teach the most able. In short, the decision about which teacher should teach which class is a professional one made by the headmaster and his staff, not something forced on them by the circumstances of selection and separation.

It is probably fair to say that "two tier" arrangements would not be popular if it were not a question of using existing buildings. The advantages claimed for it are that the full 11 to 18 age range is too wide to be successfully accommodated in one school, so separating the younger from the older makes it easier to treat each more appropriately. The two tier system does involve a second change of school quite early, after only two or three years, and this can be a hindrance unless there is very close collaboration between the two schools.

The "middle" school system, on the other hand, can be said to have very positive educational advantages. The Plowden committee on primary education recommended that the age of transfer to secondary schools should be raised to 12, and added there were nearly as many arguments for 13. They envisaged that primary education should then be divided into "lower" and "middle" schools. For this they offered a number of educational arguments. The methods which have been used with such success in primary schools can be continued into the secondary stage, and subjects like languages which have hitherto been taught only in secondary schools can be introduced at the primary stage. Schools in which pupils start at 12 or 13 can be much more "adult" institutions. Authorities using a middle school system have found it convenient to use former grammar schools as senior schools and the former secondary moderns as "middle" schools.

Those authorities which have chosen sixth form colleges have also turned grammar schools into the colleges. The advantages of this system are that the sixth formers can work in an institution designed specifically for them, and where teachers are very scarce, the sixth form work can be concentrated. The disadvantages are that sixth formers and their teachers are cut off from younger pupils and the need to transfer to another school at the school leaving age may disincline pupils from staying on.

We must now look briefly at "interim" arrangements which the Circular 10/65 said may be used to help an authority to go properly comprehensive eventually. These involve some variation of a system which was evolved in the county of Leicestershire and was known as the Leicestershire scheme. In this system all pupils transferred to comprehensive schools at 11, but those whose parents intended to keep them at school until the age of 16 were transferred to a "grammar" school at 14. The others remained in the old school. Sometimes this school offered courses leading to external examinations, sometimes it did not. A variant of the Leicestershire scheme was that all pupils transferred again at 13 or 14, some to schools for those staying well beyond the school leaving age some to those for children leaving as soon as possible. The circular said that both of these systems retain some element of selection and were thus not acceptable long term solutions.

All these systems are being used in some part of the country or other. And they are all in various stages of completion. Change will be the most obvious thing about secondary schools for many years to come, and people who travel from one part of the country to another will meet very different arrangements. In some places they will find selection still being used, though it will gradually disappear. Elsewhere they will come across perhaps unfamiliar kinds of comprehensive schools. But the point is that all the schools will eventually be comprehensive. Once you abolish selection at 11, it becomes very much less important to have the same pattern of secondary education in every local authority in the land. A genuine variety is emerging which was not possible under the old arrangements.

In the Appendix you will find a list of all the local authorities in England and Wales. Alongside each is a note saying which kind of scheme of comprehensive education they have got or are planning and the progress they have made towards its completion. This gives some idea of the way in which the method and timing of reorganization depends upon each individual local education authority.

There is one further complication. Some schools, mostly church schools, have what is known as 'aided' status. Though maintained by local education authorities they are controlled by their own boards of governors. Bringing them into a scheme of reorganisation involves the agreement of their governors and hence protracted negotiation.

To sum up, the educational case for comprehensive schools is that only in this way is it possible to give a genuine secondary education for all children. Selection has been seen to be an unnecessary mistake—not only by parents, but by educators and administrators. But education is a local concern in Britain, so the way that each area is going comprehensive depends upon its local education authority.

Note

As this book was going to press the Government introduced a Bill to speed comprehensive reorganisation. If passed it will be known as the Education Act 1970. Its first clause requires local education authorities to have regard to the need for securing that secondary education is provided in non-selective schools-with a view to ending the selection of pupils for secondary schools by reference to ability or aptitude. Exceptions are special schools, sixth form colleges and music, dancing and other art schools.

The second clause enables the Secretary of State to require a local education authority to prepare and submit plans showing how secondary education is to be provided in non-selective schools; and clause three makes it possible for both existing and future plans to be revised.

CHAPTER TWO

Transfer to secondary education

For most parents, the first official notice they have of secondary schools is probably a letter from the chief education officer in perhaps the January of their child's last year at primary school. This letter tells them that their child will be transferring to secondary school in the following September and sets out the arrangements the local authority has made. Here is the letter which Mr. H. S. Thompson, the chief education officer for Bristol, sent to parents living in areas served by comprehensive schools:

January 1968

Dear Parent,

Transfer to Secondary Education in September 1968

Your child will be of age to transfer to a secondary school next September and I am enclosing a leaflet to explain the arrangements for the transfer of children to secondary schools maintained by the Education Committee.

The majority of children in Bristol live in areas which are served either by comprehensive schools or by groups of schools organized on a comprehensive basis. These schools admit all children living in their own areas without any kind of selection test and provide a wide range of courses, including a general course of secondary education, courses having a practical bias, and academic courses leading to certificates such as the GCE at ordinary and advanced level.

The area in which you are living is served by the school shown on the form attached to this letter and your child will be able to transfer to this school next September. I shall be glad if you will complete the form and return it to the Head of your child's *present* school this week so that appropriate arrangements can be made. Later on, the Head of the secondary school will let you have further information on matters you will need to know.

If you have a particular reason for requesting the transfer of your child to a different comprehensive school, the enclosed form gives you an opportunity of stating such a preference, with the reasons for it. You will see that the possibility of such a choice being met will depend upon room being available in the school chosen. Where it is possible to meet a parent's request for a child to be transferred to a school other than the neighbourhood school a travel allowance will be paid if the distance is over the statutory three miles.

If there is anything about this letter which is not clear, or any further point about which you would like to have information or advice, please consult the Head of your child's present school.

Yours faithfully,

A similar letter was also sent to the parent living in the few areas still served by selective schools. The leaflet which was enclosed gave a full account of the arrangements in all areas of Bristol, including the possibilities for parental choice. A further letter was sent in June, telling parents at which school admission for their children had been arranged and asking them to sign a form of acceptance.

Not all authorities are able to offer the same kind of choice as Bristol, and parents are often unclear about their right to choose a particular school. Some parents, who have been dissatisfied with the school to which a local authority has allocated their child, have gone to law about it—and discovered that the law is not much help.

Let us look first at what the law says, in Section 76 of the Education Act, 1944.

76. *Pupils to be educated in accordance with the wishes of parents.*

In the exercise and performance of all powers and duties

conferred and imposed on them by this Act the Minister and local education authorities shall have regard to the general principle that, so far as is compatible with the provision of efficient instruction and training and the avoidance of unreasonable public expenditure, pupils are to be educated in accordance with the wishes of their parents.

It is important to see what this Section does *not* say! It does not say that pupils *must* be educated in accordance with the wishes of their parents. It does not even say that the authorities must follow the principle that they should. It lays down a general principle to which the authorities must "have regard", and the courts have decided that the authorities can have regard to other things as well, and can make exceptions to the general principle if they like. If a local authority says your child is to go to a certain school it is impossible to prove that they have not had regard to the general principle set out in Section 76. Indeed, it is not clear that the Section refers to choosing a school at all, but simply to what happens inside schools. The Section was slipped into the Act in the House of Lords more to soothe religious susceptibilities than anything else. And of course, we have still to mention those two hefty qualifications about efficient instruction and unreasonable expense!

But if the legal rights of parents to choose one school rather than another seem a trifle flimsy, in practice parents do have quite a bit of choice. The Department of Education and Science has published a Manual of Guidance on choice of schools which sets out "some of the relevant considerations which may need to be balanced against each other before a decision is reached." In practice these "considerations" have come to be recognised as reasonable grounds for choosing one school rather than another. They include religion, language (Welsh medium schools, for instance), traffic dangers, medical grounds, coeducation, special courses and advanced work, the provision of school meals and family associations.

The end of selection at 11 plus greatly improves the possibility of choice. Under the old system, it was no use a parent choosing a grammar school if his child did not get a high enough score in the tests. Often there was only one grammar school available and no real choice among secondary moderns. But with all schools offering a full secondary range of courses, it becomes possible for parents to have a real choice, among equal schools, between denominations, different kinds of course or for coeducation.

Take the position in Bristol again. Here all the secondary schools will increasingly offer a wide range of secondary courses. But Withywood school is strong in modern languages, Hengrove has a new arts block, Henbury is strong in music, Brislington in mathematics. St. Mary Redcliffe and Temple school is a Church of England School. So a Bristol child who is nuts about music, Italian, the drama or relativity can choose a school that is really good at it. If the school is too far from home, the authority will take him by bus.

Probably most local authorities would be only too pleased if they could offer this sort of choice to parents. The main reason why they may refuse a parent's request for a particular school is that they have some sort of "zoning" arrangements. Even in Bristol, choice depends on there being places available. To prevent one's school being overcrowded while another has empty places, an authority may allocate catchment areas or "zones" to each school. They may then make difficulties about children going to schools in other zones. The Manual of Guidance recognises that this may be necessary, but it does assume that local authorities will zone only when necessary, will stop when the need is past and will take traffic dangers, denominational preferences and exceptional circumstances into account.

A few parents cannot be convinced by the local authority's decision and ask how they can fight it. The best advice is "don't". You can go through the performance of keeping the child at home, thus forcing the authority to issue a school attendance order. You will then have the right to nominate the school named in the order for your child to attend. Only if the authority can prove that your chosen school is unsuitable for the child or would cause unreasonable public expense can they appeal to the Secretary of State to overrule your choice. But by doing this you make the child a pawn in a protracted war of attrition. Almost any school is preferable to that.

But let us assume that all goes well, as it normally does. The letter from your chief education officer will have given you some idea of what secondary schools are available. If you have any questions, or need advice, the best person to see first is the headmaster, or headmistress, of your child's primary school. He will be able to discuss your questions with your child in mind. If necessary he will be able to tell you if there is anyone else you should see or write to. You may already know something about the local secondary schools. Usually schools aquire reputations of some sort, but do not be too ready to accept the local gossip. Reputations can often be seriously out of date: a formerly enterprising school may be going through a bad patch; a once depressed school may be succeeding with new methods and approaches.

Parents have a genuine difficulty here: few people will tell them the whole truth! Education officers will rarely admit that one of their schools is better or worse than the others. Head and other teachers may feel bound by professional loyalty. Parents may be more dogmatic than informed. An inquiring parent may have to sift a good deal of fact and opinion before coming to a conclusion. And remember that you are not choosing a school in the abstract. You are choosing a school for a particular child. Any school, however splendid its local reputation, fails with some pupils. Many schools which have been sneered at have done more than their duty by individual children.

What are some of the things you should look for when trying to choose a school? Every parent will have his own ideas of what he thinks important, and nobody can do the job of choosing for you. But many parents find it helpful to have a list of things to be thinking about.

Let us assume that selection has been abolished in your area and there are a number of comprehensive schools to which your child might go. Perhaps the first thing to do is find out what sorts of schools they are. Do they take the children from 11 to 18, or do the children change schools at 13, 14 or 16? Most people do not mind if or when changes like this take place, but you might. You might believe, for example, that it is a good thing for young people to be in sixth form colleges, rather than in schools with younger children. You may be a member of a church or faith, and in this case it could be important to seek a church school or to find out what the attitude of the school is to religion. By law all schools have to offer a daily act of worship and religious instruction, but there are lots of ways of doing it. Some parents believe very strongly in co-education—others in schools for boys (or girls) only. There is a little evidence that coeducational schools are best for girls, but not enough to worry you if you have strong feelings against them. Then there is the possibility that your child has a special interest, like languages or art. You could see whether there is a local school which does this partic-ularly well. Do not forget the "out-of-school activities". These may be sports or clubs that operate during the lunch hour or after the main school day is over. Some schools have dozens of such clubs, and they can often be the mark of a lively school. Some parents are most interested in the "tone" of a school. This can mean two things: first, the atmosphere of the place. A lot contributes to this: the attitudes of the head and staff, their methods of discipline, their methods of teaching and so on. Some parents prefer a formal atmosphere, with classes streamed by ability, and so on, in the interests, perhaps, of examination success. Others go for a more relaxed or experimental approach. It can make an enormous difference to a child, so it helps to find out.

By "tone" some parents mean the preservation or improvement of accents, speech and behaviour. They like the school to be full of children like their own—or like they wish their own would be! Others think it right for schools to have children of different classes and races, with different attitudes and vocabularies. These parents seldom regard small childish obscenities as of much consequence.

All these differences are between kinds of schools: the schools themselves may be good or bad. The things that affect the quality of schools are mainly the buildings and the staff. Three quarters of the country's secondary school pupils are in places provided since the war, so the number of real slums is relatively small. And even 100 year old buildings can house educational excellence. The staff are more important, and more difficult to find out about. But many schools issue a prospectus, and headmasters normally give a report at speech day.

A thing to worry about is too rapid a change of staff. If you know that a staff is either very old or very young, but with few in between, you can suspect rapid turnover. Another important consideration is the range of subjects available. This again will depend upon the staff and their qualifications. Unfortunately the only public guide to academic standards is success in external examinations, like the GCE or CSE. But lots of examination passes do not necessarily make a good school.

Many of these questions can be answered by talks with other parents—but there really is no substitute for visiting a school. The time to go is when the school is in session, but that, of course, is when the head is busiest; so ring up and fix an appointment.

Some schools take the initiative in meeting parents, but most do not. In some areas, children from primary schools are taken by their teachers to spend half a day in the secondary schools to which they will be going in the following year. Then the secondary schools themselves may send a note to parents inviting them to visit the schools. Or the heads of local secondary schools may attend parents' meetings at the primary schools. If you are lucky you may be offered one or more of these arrangements. In most places you may not, but do not be disheartened: you can do a lot on your own, though it takes more time and trouble.

It is hardly necessary to say that the kind of contact with parents that the most thoughtful schools offer is a great help, both to parents and children, if the change from one school to another is not going to be simply bewildering. The children can meet the change of school with confidence and enjoyment, and parents can give them the kind of un-obtrusible support which is impossible if they themselves are in the dark.

It comes as a great surprise to many parents to find that the primary school teachers are often as ill-informed about the secondary schools as they are. Sometimes they cannot answer even quite simple questions. At the same time, the secondary school teachers tend to plunge into their syllabus without discovering what their pupils have done in the primary schools. The lack of contact between the two stages of education, primary and secondary can be total. And some parents see their children disturbed or dis-heartened in what should be the new adventure of the secondary school.

The Plowden Report, *Children and their Primary Schools*, discussed contacts between teachers at the point of transfer to secondary education. The report thought that this sort of contact might be increasing, but felt there was still a long way to go. In particular it asked for an interchange of knowledge about pupils and some consistency in methods of work and organization between primary and secondary schools.

Let us again assume that things go well. Your child is to go to a school that you are happy about, and he sets off on his first morning in a secondary school. He himself may have mixed feelings. Children like novelty and change and are stimulated by it. The transfer to the "big school" is something of a landmark in the process of growing up. He may be looking forward to the different subjects of the secondary stage. He is leaving the "kids" school behind. But he would not be human if he were not also a little apprehensive. It is, after all, a new experience. The secondary school will be larger and perhaps more imper-sonal. Instead of being one of the big boys in a small school he will be among the smallest boys in what may seen to be a very large one. There will be new teachers and a new building to get to know, new customs to conform to. Instead of having one teacher for most lessons, he may find he has a different teacher for each subject.

Many of the other children in his class will of course have been with him at primary school, but some may not—especially if the secondary school takes children from a number of primary schools. The problem for his teachers will be to carry on from where the primary schools left off, trying not to repeat what is already known or to jump too far ahead. This is all the more difficult if the children come from a number of schools and have reached different stages or been taught by differing methods. It is this sort of problem which makes contact between the primary and secondary school so important.

It may help in all this for the secondary school to have a written record of each child from the primary school. Practice in this matter varies enormously. In many areas nothing goes with the child to the new school. Some teachers feel that the children should have a completely fresh start, without their previous record to inhibit them.

The Plowden Report thought that schools ought to give new thought to this question, and suggested that there should be a folder for each child containing medical records and facts about illness, results of intelligence and other tests, examples of the child's work and names of books he had read, full notes of personal handicaps or special gifts, and a pen picture of the child. But the report recognised that this written record would be of limited value unless the teachers in the schools knew each other.

It may be that some of the reluctance of primary school teachers to make their records available stemmed from the fact of selection tests at 11 plus. They may have felt that it was a misuse of their records to use them to affect a child's whole future. Now that selection at 11 is disappearing teachers in both primary and secondary schools can see themselves better as engaged in cooperating in the education of the children. As they go through schools children are constantly being assessed and re-assessed. We shall see later some of the ways in which schools do this and how they organize themselves to accommodate the children's needs. What the school is trying to do, all the time, is to see how each child is getting on. All schools have to decide what work is suitable for what pupils. Right at the beginning of the secondary school it is hard for the school to test pupils. One head has said that this simply tests "what children had forgotten in the holidays." So some help from the primary school is essential if the job is to be done well.

For the present, however, we must leave the mechanics of transfer from one school to another, and look more closely at the pupils who are being transferred.

CHAPTER THREE

Children and young people

So far this book has been about the reasons for changing secondary education and what rights parents have to choose among the new secondary schools. But of course education is about children and their growth and development. It succeeds or fails with individuals, not with systems. So before we go on to look at the schools, we must understand their pupils. And the pupils, at the secondary stage of education, are going through a particularly turbulent time. From eleven or twelve onwards boys and girls embark upon those physical, mental and emotional changes that we call adolescence. They develop from childhood to maturity. And it is during these years that they are at secondary school: indeed one of the earliest Government reports on secondary education was called *The Education of the Adolescent* for this very reason. We shall all, parents, teachers and administrators get even the new secondary schools wrong if we fail to understand what are the needs of their pupils and how they can best be met.

Oddly enough it is only very recently that people have thought it necessary to know how children grow in order to educate them. Education has been a largely hit and miss affair. Even now we know next to nothing about the development of the brain after the age of about two years old. And all schools offer regular physical education without anyone's being sure whether prolonged or repeated exercise has any permanent effect on the size or strength of muscles. There is also a resistance, among educators, even to what we do know: changes have been accepted fairly quickly in primary schools for the younger children. They have been admitted much more slowly if at all in secondary schools.

So let us start with the most obvious facts. At adolescence boys and girls grow faster than they did when younger. This is known to biologists as the "adolescent spurt". Children from about four onwards grow at a fairly regular rate, that is by about the same amount (or slightly less) each year. But at adolescence they suddenly shoot up: growing half as fast again as they did in the years before. This spurt takes place in different parts of the body at different times: the leg length reaches its peak first, followed in a few months by the breadth of the body and then by the length of the trunk. It is not only the skeleton that "spurts"; the muscles do so a little later. As you might expect all this leads to a marked increase in athletic ability, especially in boys. The heart, like any other muscle, grows more rapidly. The strength of muscles increases sharply, so does the capacity of the lungs.

A lot of parents get worried about these very rapid changes. They talk about boys "outgrowing their strength". There is no scientific basis for this idea: a boy's strength increases rapidly throughout adolescence even though its period of fastest growth follows that of height. This may mean that for a short time a boy may not have the strength of the young adult he outwardly resembles—but he is much stronger than he himself was earlier. It is not only in size that boys and girls change at adolescence. They change their shape too. As children boys and girls are very similar in shape: after adolescence boys have the wider shoulders of a man, girls the broader hips of a woman.

Physical change at adolescence is not confined only to size and shape. There are also the familiar changes related to sexual development. In boys, it is the testicles whose growth quickens first, followed (alongside the height spurt) by pubic hair, the beginnings of a beard and hair under the arms. The growth of the penis also occurs alongside the height spurt and the voice breaks a little afterwards. For girls, the beginnings of growth of the breast are the normal first signs of puberty. Menarche, or the first menstrual period, nearly always occurs after the peak of the height spurt. The full reproductive function is attained perhaps a year or eighteen months later.

It is well known that girls reach adolescence earlier than boys. In girls, the height spurt takes place, on average, from $10\frac{1}{2}$ to 13; in boys from $12\frac{1}{2}$ to 15. Before adolescence boys are very little larger than girls, so the girl's adolescent spurt soon carries them past the boys and they are consequently bigger than boys (on average) between $10\frac{1}{2}$ and 13. The boys catch up and pass the girls when their own adolescent spurt begins to take effect and they end up, as adults, some ten per cent taller. Similarly girls' breasts begin to develop, on average, at 11; a boy's penis at 13.

But all this relates to average boys and girls. Individual children may differ widely in the age at which they reach puberty. For example, although the average boy begins his height spurt at 13, individual boys may start as early as $10\frac{1}{2}$ or as late as 16. Although the average age of menarche is 13, for some girls it may occur at 10—or $16\frac{1}{2}$. And it is important to remember that these variations are entirely normal; both early and late maturing boys and girls can be needlessly miserable about themselves at this stage. But it is clear that an early maturing boy may have completed his adolescence before a late maturing one has even started. Take two 14 year old boys. One may be small, with childish muscles, a smooth face and a high piping voice. The other may be practically a grown man with broad shoulders a beard and a base voice. Both are 14, and normal.

These physical changes at adolescence and the differences between individual children have important consequences for education. And they are even more important since they are matched by changes in intellectual and emotional development which are seen at the same time. Regrettably little interest has been shown in this by educators in Britain, but studies elsewhere suggest that children who are physically advanced for their age do also score higher in mental ability tests than those of the same age who are less mature. In Britain it has been discovered that early maturers gained significantly more success at 11 plus than late maturers. Not only were their test papers better: teachers' reports favoured them too. (Many local authorities make allowance for age in marking 11 plus tests, but they do not allow for early development!)

What is likely is that certain mental functions cannot take place until the brain has sufficiently matured. Most students of child development now accept that the capacity to think formally and logically comes only with adolescence and depends on the maturing of the brain and nervous system.

Similarly what little evidence there is supports the common sense idea that emotional development is related to physical changes. It is not only that a later maturing boy or girl may become worried that he or she may never develop properly—though adolescence is a time of intense concentration upon the body and of concern about its development. It must also be that the development of adult emotions depends upon the attainment of adulthood and of adult sexuality in particular.

What follows from all these facts? Perhaps the most important lesson for education is that each child is unique. True, all children grow and develop in the same way and in the same sequence, but they do so at different rates. Some develop early and some late. What is more, there are particular stages of growth where boys and girls become capable of new mental and physical activities for the first time. It is important that they should remain in contact with education beyond those moments. For one of the most heartening lessons of recent research is that education makes a difference. It is possible to enhance a child's development and improve his educational performance. At one time people used to argue passionately about whether children owed more to heredity or to environment—to nature or to nurture as it was quaintly put. This argument was important because if a child's possibilities were determined by heredity there was not much that education could do for him; if by environment, then education could make a difference. It is now thought that the matter is more complicated than the old argument allowed for. A child's characteristics are due not only to heredity, nor only to

environment—nor indeed to a mere mixture of the two—
but to the interaction between heredity and environment.
An example will make this clear. A child may inherit a
tendency to a height of six feet, but if he is badly under-
nourished he may never attain it. On the other hand if his
inheritance is for shortness no amount of feeding will make
him attain six feet! So although education may not abolish
differences in ability, it can and does improve individual
abilities.

There is one particular change in all children which many
people put down to changes in environment, and that is the
noticeable tendency in all western countries for children to
mature earlier. They are getting older younger. The age of
menarche is getting earlier by about four months every ten
years: so a girl today may expect to menstruate about ten
months earlier than her mother did. Children are also
taller and heavier today—and they may be more intelligent
too.

All this influences, or should influence, what we do in
schools. Most people would probably agree that children
should not go into the adult world until they have achieved
their adult size and strength. This means keeping the
average girl at school until past 14 and the average boy until
past 16. Any one school leaving age must be a very rough
approximation to the needs of children, but it is fairly clear
that there are good physical arguments for keeping young
people in the education system until 16—which is the
school leaving age proposed for 1972–73, when it will
replace 15. There are other educational reasons too: there
are a number of fundamental skills which cannot be taught
until adolescence. The development of strength and
muscles enables young people to be taught new physical
skills, to work to fine limits, in ways that as children they
could not. Similarly, formal thought becomes possible at
adolescence: before that stage children quite literally
cannot be taught to think. Nor, until adolescence, can the
whole range of adult emotions and behaviour become
known to them. If children leave school before adolescence
is complete they leave with an education appropriate only

to a child. After it, they can be offered an education appropriate for a young adult. Education through adolescence means an education for men and women.

But the facts of growth should lead us to be careful how we offer this education. In the first place we should distrust age-bound stages, like the 11 plus or the school leaving age. We have already seen how the 11 plus favours early maturers. Similarly, a single school leaving age is bound to be nonsensical for individual children. In part, this implies treating each child as the unique person he is. Many secondary schools have been slow to see this. The demands of the syllabus have often seemed to have over-riding importance. In primary schools teachers are increasingly coming to see that this can destroy the whole purpose of education. Gradually, in the secondary schools, children are also being encouraged to work at their own pace, to follow their own interests, to develop their own capacities. The secondary schools too will change: gradually the rigid divisions of the timetable into "subjects" will loosen; lessons will resemble lectures less and projects more. Formal instruction will look increasingly historic. Something of this is already happening, especially with older pupils, as we shall see. The schools are coming to understand that although it is right that a young man should stay in education until after adolescence, it need not be right for him to be in the atmosphere of a school. He is developing not only adult capacities but adult interests. A number of young people are already "voting with their feet" in this respect and leaving school for the local technical college. Clearly there is room for the greatest flexibility as the school leaving age approaches, and some schools are adopting it. Their pupils may spend as much time outside the school buildings, on projects and visits, as inside. The Government is beginning to discuss ways of making it possible to continue compulsory education in colleges rather than schools. So the need to educate each child as an individual is affecting even so formal a requirement as the age of compulsory education.

The differences in individual abilities and interests also

demands a wider range of facilities in schools. In part the secondary schools have always offered this. The increased space for games which is provided at least in most new schools, the workshops, craft rooms, gymnasia witness the need to meet the demands of physical development. Similarly the widening range of subjects, into more serious science, mathematics, foreign languages attest the increased intellectual capacities of the pupils. But it is important to remember that the schools are offering these opportunities to more and more children, whose needs are even more varied. This is why the greatest ranges of choice can be offered in the larger schools, why (even without reorganization) schools would tend to grow in size. A large school can offer each individual a very much larger range of possibilities than a small one.

Finally, the new secondary schools are educating young adults. So we shall see the pupils themselves taking more responsibility for their own courses, and having accommodation to match their new status. This is not just the luxury it looks to some parents. It is an essential element in meeting the needs of the young people themselves.

The schools are changing. In some ways they are not changing fast enough. But in so far as they are changing it is in response to the known needs of their pupils. We know that adolescence is a time of upheaval—but also of great potential. We know that children differ enormously in the rate at which they grow and develop. We are coming to understand how to offer education, not to age-groups, but to individuals. We are taking seriously at last the education of all young adults, not just the very bright or the middle class. What is going on in the new secondary schools may puzzle some parents. But they will be less puzzled if they remember what happens at adolescence.

CHAPTER FOUR

Entering the new secondary school

Let's suppose that your son or daughter is now going off to his new secondary school. You know about how the schools are being reorganized so as to abolish selection, and you may in fact have had some choice in the school he is now entering. You know also, in general terms, what the school will be trying to do. But what will school be like for him?

In the first place the school is likely to be bigger, perhaps very much bigger, than his primary school. Most primary schools have between 100 and 300 pupils—and there are more with fewer than 100 than with over 300. Most secondary schools have between 300 and 800 pupils, and nearly one in four of all secondary schools have more than 600. Comprehensive schools, in particular, tend to be large: more than one in four of them have more than 1,000 pupils. This can be both a challenge and a difficulty to the children. Most children like change and look forward to it. Transfer to the "big school" is almost as important a stage in growing up as starting at school in the first place. Entering secondary school can seem, literally, like entering a larger world. Children often exaggerate and boast about how different it all is from the "kids' place" they have just left.

The sense of novelty is likely to be increased by the fact that your child's secondary school is just as likely to be in a new building as not. Over half the children now in secondary schools are in schools built since the war. Something like one in five of them are in schools built since 1960. This is in marked contrast to the primary schools: only one in three primary school children are in schools built since the war. This means that for a great many children, going to secondary school may mean going from an old school building to a new one. And so far I have been talking only about whole new schools. If you count the new places added to older schools, for extensions, alterations or remodelling, then over three quarters of all the children in secondary schools are in places provided since the war. One important consequence of this is that the schools your children go to look quite different from the one you yourself attended. A great deal has happened to the design of school buildings in the last 20 years, and one of the first things that may puzzle parents as they approach the new secondary schools is simply that schools look and feel quite different. Your son, however, will not be aware of this: what he will notice is that the school is bigger and perhaps newer than the one he has just left.

What is more, the organization of it will probably be different too. In his primary school he probably stayed with one teacher for most of the day, going to another perhaps for physical education or music, but not necessarily. In the secondary school he will certainly be allocated to a class or "form". What this means in practice varies from school to school. Normally it means that there is a particular classroom in the school which is his form room, where he has a desk in which he will keep his books, papers and instruments. This room will also be the headquarters of his form master. But the boy may not actually have lessons in this room nor be taught by his form master. He will go to other masters for different subjects in their own specialist rooms.

We have seen that the secondary schools are, typically, large schools. This means that there is likely to be many more than one form in the first year. (Pupils and teachers often call the whole of a year group a form, too, which can be confusing: a "first former" is simply a boy in the first year at school). Indeed many local authorities use the number of forms there are in the first year as a handy measure of the size of the school. If 240 pupils go up from a number of primary schools to a particular secondary school, they are likely to be divided into eight forms of 30 children each. So your son is likely to be in form 1A, 1B . . . or 1H, and in an "eight form entry" school.

This dividing up may be done in different ways. One way might be to take the list of 240 children in alphabetical order and draw a line under every 30th child. Or you might pick each form out with a pin. Most often, however, the division into forms is done by some measure of ability. Where this is done it is called streaming. All it means is that the brightest children are chosen for form 1A, the next brightest for 1B and so on to form 1H, 1J or 1N. Sometimes this process is disguised by giving the classes random letters or their form master's initials, so that Mr. Wilmott, who has the brightest class, will have 1W, while Mr. Bernstein, who has the least bright, will have 1B.

It must be said at once that there is a very great deal of argument indeed about streaming by ability in this way. Probably most teachers are in favour of it. They argue that if you have 30 children, all of very differing abilities, it is very hard indeed to teach them as a group. The bright ones will be wanting to forge ahead, those in difficulty will be lagging behind and both will be neglected while the teacher goes at the pace of the majority. In other words, forms of mixed ability handicap the teacher and are unfair to many children.

On the other hand some teachers doubt whether in mixed groups the bright are necessarily held back and the least bright neglected. They argue that it is a matter of how you teach: if teaching methods allow for individual pupils to work at their own pace there is no need for difficulty. Streaming, these teachers argue, is very bad for the less bright children, who may get demoralised and disaffected. The argument is by no means settled yet: there is nowhere near enough research evidence on the question. In Britain most secondary schools are streamed: abroad fewer are. Some schools have a variation of streaming in the first or second year. They may make up one form of pupils who are obviously very bright, another of those who are in educational difficulty, and then sort out the rest at random. This means, in effect that most forms have a very broad range of ability (though not the very brightest or the least bright) with two "special" forms at each end. Schools which do this claim that they gain the major advantages of streaming without the disadvantages: most children are after all neither very bright nor very dull.

But how are the children measured by ability by their first day at school? Parents may well ask. Where the 11 plus procedure still occurs (which is in most places) there is a ready made ranking which can be used. Sometimes the secondary schools test the pupils the moment they arrive, though we have noted one head's description of this as "testing what they have forgotten during the holidays" and it penalises those children whose primary schools do not happen to have covered the right ground for the test. In some areas, a record on each child is sent from the primary schools to their secondary schools.

Some people feel that comprehensive reorganization really implies the end of streaming too. They feel that the arguments for selective schools and for streaming are the same: are, in fact, equally good or bad depending which side they are on. There is a lot of needless confusion about this because people use the word "selection" to describe both streaming and the 11 plus. There is no need to argue merely about words and definitions. Selection at 11 plus has always meant selection for different kinds of schools. What happens inside schools is another matter: as we have seen most schools "select" in the sense that they stream their pupils by ability. But it is not right for either the defenders or the opponents of selection to argue that there is no change if after comprehensive reorganization schools still stream. The point is that selection at 11 plus is an administrative act and children go to physically different schools as a result of it. Transfer from one school to another is rare. In a single comprehensive school, streaming (which may indeed be very rigid, and transfer between streams rare) is a device decided upon by the head teacher and his staff. If they change, or change their minds, they can change their organization. The division of pupils by ability becomes then a professional matter for the teachers in the school, according to their own best judgment in their own unique circumstances.

Dividing children into forms, whether by ability or not, is not the only sort of division your son or daughter may meet with in the new secondary school. Another common device is to superimpose upon the basic division further divisions for particular subjects. The argument for this is that among children of very similar overall ability some may be good at mathematics, others at modern languages and so on. So for these subjects they are redivided according to their ability in those particular subjects. These groups are often called "sets". Sometimes, if a school has the staff it may divide the whole first year into more sets than there are forms. So your son may be in Form 1D, in set 1:1 for modern languages, because he is good at French; in set 1:8 for mathematics because he is poor at that; and set 1:4 for science, because he is average there. Sometimes setting involves choice. In any one year there may be a choice between two languages or two approaches to science, or between two quite different subjects. There may, for example, be only one set in every year which does Latin and those pupils in the Latin set may have to give up metalwork or geography. All this may seem confusing to take in all at once. Most secondary school children become quite familiar with it in a day or two.

There is a further division, which has nothing to do with ability and may have little to do with classwork. It assumes a particular importance in large schools. This is the "house" system. As its name implies it derives from boarding schools, where houses are often just that: the places where the pupils live and sleep. They are less appropriate, often, in day schools—particularly if the schools have not been built round houses and the latter have therefore no physical headquarters. In most secondary schools children are divided at random into four, or six, houses—whose purpose is most obvious on sports days or games matches or other competitive occasions. But some schools use the house system to break the school into smaller units, to try to see that every child is known well by at least one member of staff who has a special responsibility for him. In these schools, the boy will have not only a form master and teachers for different subjects, but a house master or house tutor as well. In these schools it may well be the house tutor who keeps track of the boy's progress throughout the school and who would be ready to give advice to him or his parents, rather than the form master. In some schools the houses have their own accommodation. They may each have a building including a dining room, used also as an assembly room, a house study room-cum-library, staff room, lockers for sports kit and books, lavatories and so on. Morning assembly might be held here, and it is here that the pupils come to change their kit and books and, in their leisure time, to play chess or table tennis or just to talk with friends. The point about the house is that it contains pupils of all ages, not just those in a year group. The older pupils will be likely to have both disciplinary and "pastoral" responsibilities.

So you can see that your son or daughter, as well as being in a bewildering number of different forms or sets, may also be in a house (called "Nelson", "Romans" or some such) to which, you may find, he owes a fair degree of loyalty.

Size and organization are not the only changes your child will notice as he goes into his secondary school. There will be, opening out in front of him, a whole new world of different subjects and interests. Of course, one must not underestimate the breadth and fascination of the curriculum in good primary schools. Indeed primary school teachers can often justly claim that they hold the interest of children better than secondary schools. But in secondary schools pupils are expected to take on a heavier load of subjects and their growing capacities, described in Chapter Three, enable them to pursue these in increasingly mature ways. The curriculum of the secondary school will be described in the following chapters. Here it is enough to indicate the experience that will greet the new pupil as he enters secondary school. The first change he may notice is the introduction of a foreign language. Most children meet a language other than their own for the first time in the secondary school. Schools may offer French, German, Spanish, Italian, Russian (a few) or even Chinese (very rare). Some schools still continue with the dead languages, Latin and Greek, because of some surviving university entry requirements. In the secondary school pupils also begin to look on their own language in a sense as "foreign": they try to understand its structure and to analyse its literature. The old familiar arithmetic branches out into new relationships in mathematics, into algebra and geometry and later trigonometry. Experiments in science become more formal, in specially equipped laboratories. Primary school tales of famous people or far off lands become history and geography: chronology is established and motives analysed; the nation's resources and wealth may begin to be understood. The school may well have large playing fields and well equipped gymnasia for the exercise of new physical strength and skill. Workshops, art and craft rooms, domestic science rooms will serve the need to create and work to fine limits. These will give the first hint of the vocational bias that most youngsters come to demand as they grow up. There may well be an extensive range of activities going on "outside the classroom" after school and in the lunch hour, in clubs and societies for everything from debating to philately.

To teach these, often unfamiliar subjects, there are specialist teachers. In some secondary schools, as in primary schools, each form may be taught by one teacher for most of the time and in most subjects, with the specialists for music or languages chipping in almost on the fringe. But in most secondary schools, each subject is increasingly being taught by a specialist. One teacher will, for example, teach history or mathematics throughout the school, to pupils of all ages, and may teach nothing else. Each lesson, a new form or set will arrive in the specialist's room, and he will change from discussing the Renaissance with the sixth form to exploring Saxon windows with the first. A specialist teacher may have a university honours degree (about a third of all secondary school teachers are graduates) or he may have taken his specialism to about pass degree standard at a college of education. (It would be fair to say here that there is an acute and growing shortage of specialists, particularly in science and mathematics, in all schools.).

So far we have been looking at the school and its teachers from the point of view of the pupils. Let us look at it, for the moment, from the point of view of the teachers. All of them will have many and varied responsibilities. For example, a man may be one of the school's science specialists, teaching pupils of all ages, from elementary to quite high levels. He will get to know these pupils as he sees them regularly and will have a good idea of their academic work in his subject. He may also be the form master of, say, one of the first forms. If he does not teach this form he may see them rarely, but he may well get to know some of them and may be the person to whom one or two of them may turn in a difficulty. He may also be a house tutor. His house group will include pupils of all ages, and he and they will remain together so long as they are at the school. He will be expected to make a particular effort to get to know them well and to be able to report not only upon their general academic progress but about their development as individuals. In addition, a teacher who is particularly interested in some activity like music, drama or sport will come across the pupils who join it after normal school hours.

More senior teachers may have added responsibilities, as house masters, for example, as heads of subject departments or as "year" masters. The house master may be responsible for the house accommodation and activity of a quarter or a third of the pupils in the school, the subject head for all the teaching in his speciality, and the "year" master for all the pupils in a particular age-group. At the head of the school is the headmaster or headmistress, often with one or two deputy heads. In large schools, the head may be a somewhat remote figure, even though some make great efforts to get to recognise individual pupils by name. But the head is a key figure. On him or her may depend the whole tone of the school, its atmosphere and attitude to work and life. A head may not do very much teaching (though some heads make a point of spending a good deal of time at it) but he can greatly affect the quality of the teaching.

What I have been saying so far applies pretty well to all schools. But of course there is a very great variety of secondary schools to which your children might go. In most local authorities, there will still be a selective process at 11 plus, and the children will find themselves in different kinds of schools; grammar, technical, secondary modern as the case may be. This book is about the new comprehensive secondary schools, but it may be as well to describe the others briefly here. Children with high ability as measured by the 11 plus tests are offered places in grammar schools. Over the country as a whole about one in four of all children go to them, though in particular areas rather more or fewer may do so. The grammar schools are devoted to an academic education and are much influenced by the requirements of universities for entry qualifications. Three quarters of their teachers are graduates: that is, they have been educated to a high level in a particular subject. Many of them have not been trained as teachers. A grammar school will expect most of its pupils to stay at school beyond the compulsory school age, to take the General Certificate of Education at the ordinary level at 16. (There is more about examinations in Chapter Eleven). They will encourage their pupils to stay a further two years for the GCE advanced level.

Most of the rest of the children will go to secondary modern schools. These vary enormously in what they are like and in what they offer. Some have tried to evolve a curriculum arising less from academic demands than from the interests of the children. Others do what they can to offer "grammar school" opportunities. Very few of their teachers (about one in six) are graduates, but most of them have been trained as teachers and will have taken one or two specialist subjects to quite a high level at college. Most pupils in secondary modern schools leave at the earliest legal age, though increasing numbers are staying on for an extra year often to take an examination. Some may take

GCE O level (but fewer than half the schools put in pupils for it) and others the new Certificate of Secondary Education. Very few secondary modern schools have large numbers staying after the age of 16.

There are also a very few technical schools, taking selected pupils at 11 plus and offering them a more industrially biassed curriculum, and a few mixed arrangements of grammar and secondary modern departments known as bilateral or multilateral schools.

Even if you live in an area where the 11 plus procedure has disappeared, you may well find a variety of schools available. As we saw in Chapter One, local authorities are reorganising their secondary schools on comprehensive lines by using existing buildings and thus a variety of methods. Your son may therefore find himself in a very large school, taking pupils from 11 to 18, or in a rather smaller one, taking pupils from 11 to 13, 14 or 15. If the latter is the case he will expect to transfer to another comprehensive secondary school later on. People often argue passionately that one or other form of arrangement is the best, but as we have seen there are arguments for and against all of them, and it is not sensible to dogmatise. The quality of education your child gets will depend mostly on the quality and personality of the head teacher and his staff, to a lesser extent on the school buildings and equipment and even less on the precise form of organization which is adopted.

Let us imagine, then, your son in his new school on the first morning, standing in his place on the school hall for assembly. Around him will be some of the friends he knew at primary school, but perhaps most of the children even of his own age will be unfamiliar to him. Behind him will be the rest of the big school, the oldest of them looking to him as adult as the teachers. In front of him on the platform the headmaster announces the hymn, the tune and words of which are strange: "Lord, behold us with thy blessing once again assembled here . . ." There will be a short prayer or two, a notice which he scarcely understands, and then he will file out to find his form room, his timetable and a new kind of school life.

What this will turn out to be is the subject of the next seven chapters. But before leaving this one, let us look at the way one comprehensive school—Gordano School in Somerset—welcomes new pupils with an account of its organization and customs. First of all there are some extracts from a booklet which all parents get shortly before their children enter.

Gordano School — The first two years.

Introduction

In September your daughter will become a member of Gordano School. This marks the beginning of an important new stage in her life, and it would be surprising if it did not raise many questions in your mind.

These notes will not answer all your questions, nor are they designed as a substitute for personal contact between you and the school. Indeed, I hope you will be able to accept the invitation to come to the school with your daughter, and that this contact, once made, will be maintained throughout your daughter's schooldays with us. The school and the home must pull in the same direction.

The information in this pamphlet will give you a picture of the school with particular emphasis on the Lower School —the first two years.

W. R. THOMAS,
Head of the Lower School.

Your Child in the School.

Gordano School is a bigger school than those from which the children have come.

The children will come into contact with new teachers, and the buildings may seem strange and rather forbidding at first. From being members of a small community, the children will find themselves members of a much larger one. There will be more movement during a school day than children have been used to as they go to specialist rooms for particular subjects. Above all, the size of the school is such that parents are very naturally concerned in case their child, as an individual, may not be known nor her interests fully met.

This is a matter to which we are very much alive. One headmaster would indeed find it difficult to know over a thousand children personally, but this is not important. What is important is that every child should be well known by someone in a senior position on the staff. This may be the Head of the Lower School, a Housemaster or Housemistress, or the Head of Upper School.

The school has therefore been organised in such a way that each pupil is known as an individual, and that her needs are met, both in her academic work and as a member of the school community.

The Organisation of the School.

When children enter the school at 11, they become members of the Lower School. The Lower School is made up of children in the first and second years. Each child is allocated to a Form in charge of a Form Master or Form Mistress who is responsible, under the general direction of the Head of the Lower School, for his welfare in all aspects of school life.

At the beginning of the third year, children move into one of five Houses. Each House is divided into five Tutor Groups consisting of about 25 to 30 children in charge of a Tutor and under the general direction of a Head of House. The Tutor Group may be likened to a family group, because the child will be with children of his own age and those who are older, as each group will include pupils in their third, fourth and fifth years.

Each Form in the Lower School and Tutor Group in the Houses meets for registration in the mornings and afternoons, as well as lunch time when the Lower School and the Houses take lunch separately.

The Lower School and Houses organise various activities, including games, and it will be seen that the smaller units within the whole school do mean that the needs of the individual child are met by staff whose special responsibility this is.

Your child's progress through the school.

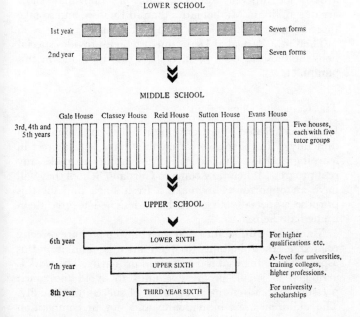

The Curriculum

In the Lower School, children will receive a broad, general education.

All children will study English, Mathematics, Science,

History, Geography, a foreign language, Religious Education, and practical subjects—Domestic Science and Needlework for the girls; Woodwork and Metalwork for the boys. In the second year, some children will be given the opportunity of starting a second language.

Although all children will follow the same curriculum, they differ in their abilities and skills, and the speed with which they can assimilate new ideas and practise new techniques. Accordingly, every effort is made to ensure that children are in a group which best suits their abilities, and this may well mean that children find themselves in different groups for different subjects. Thus a child may show greater ability in Mathematics than in English, and so take these subjects with different groups of pupils.

There is a Remedial Department which provides special help for those in need of it. Details will be found in this pamphlet.

The Remedial Department.

For various reasons, there are children who have found such difficulty with school work that they have lost interest in learning and lost confidence in their ability to make any real progress. When they come to Gordano School they will have an opportunity to make a fresh start, and for this purpose a special course has been designed to give them immediate help.

Many of the difficulties that the children face are directly related to their inability to read fluently, and it is this aspect of learning that is emphasised primarily. The work is arranged in small, progressive units to avoid too much pressure, and to ensure a measure of success continually. The children work individually and not in competition with others. This enables them to advance independently according to the amount of time and effort they are prepared to spend on their work. Parents are invited to take a practical interest in the work that the children do, although it must be understood that the effort must come from the pupils: parents and teachers help.

Since Gordano School caters for the full ability range and allows easy transfer from group to group, no limit is placed on how much progress a child may make, though no promises can be made in predicting what that progress will be. However, it can be safely said that a child is most likely to succeed when he

(a) is sure of affection, understanding and good discipline,

(b) appreciates that parents and teachers are working together for his benefit,

(c) feels that he is as important as anyone else, but no more,

(d) knows that he is making progress in work that interests him.

In everyday terms, every child should have the security of a healthy daily routine (e.g. regular and punctual attendance, sensible bedtime, time for work and play), encouragement from parents and teachers (e.g. interest shown in their homework, permission to join clubs, praise for good work), and possession of the ordinary things that, most children have (e.g. uniform, satchel, games kit writing equipment).

The School always welcomes the co-operation of parents, never more so than when the children's welfare is at stake. Every child entering the first-year remedial class should have as his motto:

'A fresh start, a fresh attitude, fresh interests'.

> T. P. Evans,
> Head of the Remedial Department.

(*There are many other sections in the booklet, on school activities and societies for example. The following are of the most general interest*).

Homework

All children will do homework, the amount varying according to their needs at each stage in their school life.

Homework provides an opportunity for children to go

more deeply into a subject, to practise a newly acquired skill, to read more widely, to consolidate new ideas and to develop self reliance by working on their own.

Parents often ask how they can help children with their homework.

First and foremost, your children will be encouraged if you take an interest in what they are doing, ask to see their books, or offer to test some work which has to be learnt.

Help the children to make a timetable, so that a routine is established leaving time when homework is done for the children to develop their interests and hobbies, which are very important to their development.

If a room can be set aside where homework can be done free from disturbance this is ideal. Such an arrangement is not always possible, but try to give them the use of a table at which they can work.

Each child will be given a homework timetable showing the subjects for the evening and the time to be spent on each. The work set for each evening has to be entered in a homework note-book with which the child is provided. Parents are asked to sign this book at the end of the week.

If you find, over a period, that homework is taking longer than it should, don't hesitate to get in touch with the school. At any time, children should consult their teachers if they have been unable to do the work set.

Uniform

The wearing of school uniform is part of the school regulations and is required by the Governors of the School. You will see that a basic uniform is specified, and this includes clothing essential for sports and gymnastics.

If you wish to buy articles of clothing in addition to those specified in the basic uniform, a recommended list is given.

The uniform list has been drawn up in consultation with the Parent–Teacher Association. After a very careful and thorough examination of school clothing, a sub-committee of the Association has recommended the articles listed on the next page. (*The list is omitted here*).

The uniform sub-committee of the Parent–Teacher Association recommend the following official suppliers of Gordano School Uniform:

(Here two names are given)

If you plan to make the summer dress, please ensure that you obtain the correct pattern and material. The pattern is BUTTERICK No. 2642, View 'A', with two modifications. The belt is fastened by two buttons and not a buckle, and the cuffs should be cut with the stripes running horizontally.

You may wish to take advantage of credit schemes in purchasing school clothing. One supplier operates a credit scheme at their Branch where enquiries should be made; the other has a Personal Budget Accounts Scheme, and details of this may be obtained from them.

The Home and the School.

The home and the school must work together. If this co-operation does not exist, the children suffer.

The school will keep you fully informed of your daughter's progress. You will be invited to the school to discuss this with the Staff at important stages in her career.

The Headmaster and Senior Staff are always willing to meet you to discuss any aspect of your child's school life. Make an appointment beforehand, either by 'phone—Portishead 3586/3587—or in writing. While your child is in the Lower School you may contact Mr. W. R. Thomas or his Assistant, Mr. L. R. Vaughan.

School Reports.

Detailed Reports on your child's progress are given twice a year—at the end of February and at the end of the Summer Term. Parents are asked to sign the reports; they will then be filed at the school.

In addition to these half-yearly reports, an initial report is issued, after the first half-term of the first year. This summarizes your child's capabilities and potential in English and Mathematics.

The School endeavours to write honest reports; only in this way can we be fully helpful, for we hope that, by keeping one another informed, parents and School can together guide children along the right lines.

We feel that information should flow in both directions, from school to home and from home to school. Just as it is important for parents to have a clear picture of how we at school see the development of their children, so we have much to learn from the parents. We should like to know, for example, about your daughter's out-of-school interests, what part she takes in community life, any problems with homework, attitudes, hopes or worries—in short, anything you feel may be of help.

It is advisable to make a note of the salient points of each report; a clearer picture of progress—or otherwise—then emerges. Do not hesitate to ask to discuss your child's report with us if you feel the need to do so.

The reports will be filed at school until the child leaves. They may be consulted by parents at any stage on request.

The Parent-Teacher Association.

As soon as your child joins the School, you will automatically be eligible to become a member of the Parent-Teacher Association.

The object of the Association is to promote activities designed to benefit the School, and therefore your child. These activities include the raising of funds to provide additional facilities, as well as meetings of a social or educational nature for the benefit of members.

The Association is run by a Committee of parents and members of staff, but any Sub-Committees it may form have the power to co-opt outside help. Your active support is needed to maintain the Association's valuable work.

The Annual General Meeting is held in or near to September, and you will be notified of the date and time in advance. Do come to this meeting.

In order to cover the normal work and maintenance of the Association, there is an Annual subscription of 1/- per family, payable on or before the date of the Annual General Meeting, and valid for the ensuing year.

A copy of the Constitution of the P.T.A. is available on request. The Officers of the Association for 1966/67 are:

(*and here the names and addresses are given*).

At the beginning of the third year, parents get another booklet, this time about the new organization and curriculum for the next three years. Some extracts from this booklet are also given here.

Gordano School — Middle School.

Years three, four and five (the Middle School).

The beginning of the third year marks an important change in the school life of a boy or girl at Gordano.

The most obvious change from Lower to Middle School is the entry into a House. Here, pupils are no longer in units of a Form of boys and girls of the same age but members of a Tutor Group where the ages range over three years. The Tutor Group is not unlike a family, whose members also vary in age, interests, and ability, and where each uses his talents to help the others; to encourage them to do this there are the House Tutor and the House Master or Mistress, both of whom take a personal interest in every boy and girl in their Group and House. They are there to advise on choice of courses, to give help with personal problems, to maintain vital contact with parents. Housemasters or mistresses, aided by their tutors, are primarily "in loco parentis" to help each boy or girl to make the most of opportunities and to guide them towards becoming

increasingly strong in character and useful members of
the community.

The Middle School is a period of transition: the transition
from childhood to young adulthood. For some, it is the final
stage of formal schooling before they take their place in the
world of work; for others, it is the preparation for higher
education in the Upper School and beyond.

For all, it is a period of important opportunities that must
be utilized to the full.

The Curriculum.

There are other changes. Apart from the different, more
adult social atmosphere of the House, pupils find an
increasing difference in the curriculum. In the third year,
they still follow a basic course, but with increased specialis-
ation: for example, in several sets General Science now
gives way to the separate disciplines of Physics, Chemistry
and Biology.

The major curricular change, however, comes in the
fourth year, when teaching staff, pupils and parents decide
courses from a considerable choice. Some of these courses,
with individual subject choice as well as a 'common core',
lead to GCE or CSE, others to a mixture, or to no examination, depending upon the aptitude and intentions of the
individual pupil. Moreover, the same target may be
achieved over various periods; different groups may, for
example, take the same examination in their sixth, their
fifth, or even their fourth year. (The latter does not apply
to CSE, for which a minimum of five years is required).

Parents will be invited to discuss the various options at the
appropriate time—e.g. towards the end of the third and
fifth years.

Examinations.

Rightly or wrongly, external examinations are a necessary

part of modern life. For entry into the professions they are essential, but also in many trades qualifications are demanded by employers. The impending raising of the school leaving age and the Industrial Training Acts make it clear that qualifications will become more, not less, important.

The main External Examinations are:

(1) The GCE (General Certificate of Education) taken at O-level (Ordinary level) in any number of subjects.

A-level (Advanced level) in one, two or three subjects in the sixth forms.

S-level (Scholarship level).

(2) The CSE (Certificate of Secondary Education).

A nationwide examination administered on a regional basis, first held in 1965. There are five pass grades, Grade 1 being recognised as the equivalent of an O level pass.

Through the system of options, each pupil has, in effect, a personal timetable from the fourth year.

To take an examination course it is, obviously, necessary to complete at least five years in school.

Non-Examination Courses.

Some children are quite unsuited to the pressures and requirements of an examination course. This is in no way a reflection on the child, his home, or his education: children are different in their needs and abilities.

For children in this group, there are courses which in some ways have little to do with conventional lessons. The problem, which was highlighted by the Newsom Report and by the Department of Education and Science's Working Paper on the Raising of the School Leaving Age (both stimulating reading for anyone interested in education), is largely one of preparing young people for entry into an adult world for which they are in many ways unprepared.

Courses are prepared, therefore, with a high practical

content and with a largely individual time-table—especially in the fifth year. It is possible that some pupils will even take one or two subjects in CSE. Again, considerable thought is put into the curriculum to make its relevance to life abundantly clear to the young person; in this, too, parents can help greatly by their encouragement and interest.

Future plans include a scheme whereby all children in a non-examination course may spend a period of time actually working in commerce or industry—for educational reasons.

Success can take many forms besides prowess in examinations.

Evans House.

Evans House was formed in September 1966 with an entry of third year boys and girls. In 1967 and 1968 our numbers will increase so that we shall have pupils of all ages and ability from the third, fourth and fifth years.

At the moment we are occupying a series of rooms in a temporary building, but in a few years' time we look forward to living in a splendid, new House with all the tasteful furnishings that the other Houses already enjoy.

However, it will be the members, and not the buildings, that will determine whether the House gains for itself a good reputation. We have made a promising start and we hope that in future years our new members will endeavour to maintain our worthwhile traditions. To this end we have adopted CHIVALRY as our watchword, a term that implies courtesy and gentleness, courage and initiative, generosity and service. We may not, always, individually, live up to these high standards, but we cannot do better, as a community, than to accept these as our beacons.

                                              T. P. Evans,
                                                    Housemaster.

Careers.

Some children know from an early age what they wish to do

(and a few do actually become engine drivers). Others are undecided till a late stage.

For both groups, in particular the latter, access to expert advice is essential. We do our best to make this advice available, both from our own resources by appointing senior staff specially trained to know the complexities of qualifications, and who can advise on the suitability of the individual for a particular career, and by bringing outside experts into school to interview pupils and their parents.

Pupils have access to this advice in the following ways:

(1) Discussions with Housemaster/mistress and tutor.

(2) Advice from subject teachers and Heads of Departments about individual subjects. For example, an early choice of a particular group of subjects may be essential for later qualification in a particular branch of study, e.g. a student intending to read Mathematics at University should opt for Physics, and so on.

(3) Talks with the Careers Master, Head of Upper School and staff on the Careers Committee.

(4) Visits to the Careers Display Room in the School.

(5) Individual and group discussions with the visiting Youth Employment Officer.

(6) Individual and group discussions with the visiting Careers Advisory Officer (for A level pupils).

(7) The possibility, for some pupils, of a residential "Learning to Earning" course.

CHAPTER FIVE

English and Mathematics

English

When a number of parents of 15 year old school leavers were asked what they thought were the most important things a school could teach, very nearly all of them said, "to be able to put things in writing easily." We shall come back to this inquiry and its results later (in Chapter Eleven), but this one reply is a good way to start talking about the teaching of English. This is the one subject which most people agree is basic to the school curriculum. Indeed, at one time schools concentrated on this and a little arithmetic —and not much else. The joke title of the "three Rs," for reading, 'riting and 'rithmetic, came to describe what some people thought schools were really about: everything else was a "frill" or was less essential. This attitude is changing fast: the other subjects of the school curriculum are being increasingly understood and accepted. The *way* in which English is taught is as important as the fact of teaching it. But parents are right when they say that a good grasp of English is a fundamental of all education. Are they also right when they (or some of them) complain that the schools neglect it these days or teach it in airy-fairy ways which do not give a good grounding in it? It is, of course, not only the organization of schools which is changing today, but also the curriculum. The subject of English, like that of mathematics, may seem very different from what parents themselves remember. Is this a bad thing? Is secondary education, for all its new buildings and organization, going to the dogs?

To answer this question, we shall have to spend a little time on discussing what English is for. Why do we teach it?

The question is a funny one in some ways, because of

course parents teach their children English from birth (at least English parents do!) It has its roots in human contact and communication. When a baby is very small, he communicates pretty inadequately. He may smile—and as every mother knows this may indicate either pleasure or just wind. He may cry—and if you watch a baby you will notice that almost the whole of his body is involved in crying: he cries, as it were, all over. And when he cries you have to discover by trial and error what is wrong. It may be cholic, or a wet nappy, or a pin sticking in. The baby cannot explain until he has a language. This is partly what the teaching of English is about: extending a child's ability to express himself through a better grasp of language. Of course, there are other ways of communicating. Gestures can be very effective: may indeed be unanswerable. Or one may communicate through painting or music. But language remains a central means for human beings.

What parents do naturally, the schools extend: and parents can encourage themselves by remembering that they are likely to have taught their children some 3,000 words before they start school. Indeed, until children have a vocabulary of roughly this size it is very difficult indeed for them to learn to read. But language is not just about words: it includes the increasingly complicated ways in which words are put together to convey more complex meaning. A baby may start with the simple syllable, "Mum". He then progresses to "my mum"—which is a much more complicated idea, involving two people and possession. To say nothing of more involved later relationships: "she shall be mine"—"be mine!"—"she was mine once"—"she might have been mine"—"she should never have said she could be mine"—and so on.

The most natural way of expressing ourselves in language is through speech. This is so obvious that people often forget it. The schools are in process of bringing back speech into the curriculum, not so that they can be taught to speak with proper accents (though some teachers no doubt try) but so that they can have the greatest possible practice in expressing themselves. This is why they are encouraged at school to talk with their teachers and with one another, to listen and be listened to, to debate and discuss, to improvise dramatic scenes and so on. It is why oral tests and examinations, for all their difficulties, are being brought back into the schools.

Now, it is clear that some people are better at talking than others. Many people are so bad at it that they distrust those who are better: to be said to have the gift of the gab is not exactly a compliment, though there is envy in the phrase. We have all been in situations where we are at a loss for words, where a readiness to speak might have made things easier. We all know people who say they would rather die than make a public speech. It is not too much to say that the tongue-tied have been very badly educated.

But if speech is the most natural way to communicate, the extensions of it, reading and writing, have been around for a very long time. Their invention extended the possibilities of communication almost infinitely. A person could communicate with others far away, whom he may not ever have met, or in enormous numbers. This function has been parallelled by radio and television. But reading and writing also meant that people could communicate much more complicated messages and ideas. A man reading a book can go at his own pace and check back on what has gone before: he can concentrate until he understands. A man listening to a speech is not so lucky: he has to keep up as best he can. This is why the most successful speeches are the simplest. This function of reading and writing—of conveying complicated information—has not yet been matched by radio and television, which in this respect are still in the stone age.

So schools teach reading and writing. The basic skills are taught in the primary schools, or should be. What the secondary school does is to give children practice at them, in ways which change with their changing interests, capacities, emotions and understanding. The kind of things they read and write will naturally be quite different at the beginning and end of their secondary schooling.

Most people read for perhaps two main reasons, for

information and for pleasure. In a daily newspaper they may get both. But a complicated society like our own depends on people being able to read. The normal business of living brings us up against notices, forms to fill in, instructions to master and so on. We do this without thinking about it much, but *if* you think about it you will realise that you scarcely move a step or pass five minutes without reading something. Most of us need more information than this, too. To learn any new subject, to master a trade or skill, to take up a hobby, all depend on reading, and do so more and more. The number of things you can be taught merely by word of mouth is getting smaller all the time. But we need more than to be able simply to take in information: for most things we also have to make decisions, about buying one brand of goods rather than another, about choosing a holiday, about voting at an election. We need to be able to read, certainly, but also to to able to read critically. What is this advertisement or that politician really saying? Are the promises quite what they seem to be? So when children read books at school they are encouraged to ask, "Is this true?"—or "Does this set out to mislead?"

But this has scarcely touched the beginnings of what reading can do. It can amuse, shock, kill time perhaps, disgust and irritate. It can make us think, introduce us to new ideas. It can arouse our imaginations, introduce us to whole worlds which we would otherwise never meet. In short, it enlarges our understanding and our experience: we can come up against situations in books and stories and poetry which we could never meet in life. And we can learn from these experiences as well, often, as we can learn from personal ones. This is what the study of literature is about in schools. Some parents cannot see why children spend their time on novels often about people from past ages or on poetry which seems to be remote from reality. But literature and poetry are about people, acting and reacting to each other in particular situations. They are about feelings and emotions. Children can learn through literature about themselves, other people, personal relationships, about possibilities and frustrations, about social pressures, about what constitutes vice or virtue. Literature, in other words, nourishes understanding and imagination. It is about people and about life. So a good part of the secondary school English curriculum will be devoted to studying stories, novels and poems.

But being educated is not only a matter absorbing experience. An essential part of it lies in expressing yourself. Of course, most people see writing as something which is mainly "useful." They can see the point of letters, job applications, jotting down lists and notes. There can be very few people who have not wished at some time in their lives to be able to make a better job of letter writing. But the capacity to write does more than this. It not only helps you to organize your thoughts: it helps you to think. There was once a man who said, "How can I tell what I think until I hear what I say?"—and he was only half joking. Thinking means putting into words: until we have the words we cannot think. The better command we have of words the better our command of ideas.

Many people can see that reading helps you to understand things better, but find it hard to believe that writing does. But perhaps most authors write in order to make themselves understand. In a sense they write for themselves and not the public. In what I write about education, the parts that give me the greatest satisfaction to do are those which enable me to understand something new. So children at school do a lot of writing, about themselves and their experiences, about their family, friends and interests. And, although they may start with their own immediate concerns, they do not stop there: they use this as a base for further exploration of the world. They write stories and poetry and all kinds of descriptions.

All this is put very briefly, but I hope it is clear why the skills of reading and writing are basic to education. Parents may still be puzzled: I have talked about English as a "skill". When we were at school English was a "subject", with things to learn in it. A noun was a naming word, an adjective a describing word, a verb a doing word and so on.

There were proper nouns (with capital letters) and common nouns (without). There were phrases and clauses, and these might be adjectival or adverbial. There were, for the more advanced, gerunds or verbal nouns. And we were set to "parse" sentences, saying which words were what "parts of speech". We learned all about punctuation and did exercises in it. Some of our teachers became quite mad about the difference between a colon and a semi-colon or had strong views about commas. Sentences always began with capital letters. And then there was spelling: we not only had periodic quizzes in it, we had to write out (often over and over again) the words we had got wrong.

If parents have any single complaint against the new secondary schools it is that all this seems to have gone by the board. "They don't teach them to spell any more", is a frequent cry, from parents and employers alike. And complaints about the standard of writing are even louder. Up to a point all this is true. There are fewer and fewer formal lessons in grammar, spelling and punctuation. Children spend little time doing the rows of elegant pot-hooks which led to copperplate script. Few teachers ignore this altogether. A child's exercise book may still have quite a number of spelling and punctuation corrections: there will still be rude notes in it about tidyness. But the teacher no longer feels, probably, that this is the main object of English teaching. He will want his pupils' writing to be legible (otherwise why write?) and the punctuation and spelling ought not to get in the reader's way either. But his main concern will be with what is written, how the thought is expressed, whether it is clear or vivid, whether it succeeds in its object—to inform, to arouse emotion or interest. For these purposes spelling and punctuation are aids, not regulations. Indeed, constant worry about them may simply freeze the ability to write at all. No child will put his mind and heart into his work if he is going simply to be nagged about whether or not i comes before e except after c. The long term objectives of English teaching are to listen and read with understanding, to speak and write fluently, clearly and creatively. And the hope is that they will go on doing this throughout life. How many of us bothered about adjectival clauses after we had left school?

But is there nothing wrong with the new methods? There must be few teachers who would claim that all is well in English. Many of the difficulties arise from the changes themselves. There are plenty of uncertainties still. Teachers are trying experiments, and some of them may turn out to be mistakes. The work of the Schools Council (of which there will be more in Chapter Thirteen) means that there are many more changes to come. Some teachers, like some parents, are still unconvinced about the new methods. Sometimes teachers and pupils have to adapt their new approaches to old style examinations. The training of teachers of English still leaves much to be desired. Many teachers who lack qualifications, interest or conviction are teaching English because there is no one else to do it. And the new methods, which are designed to stretch the abilities, imagination and understanding of the pupils can be pretty demanding on the teachers too. In some places they are trying to do their new and enlarged job with poor stocks of books, poor libraries and cramped accommodation.

But the main fear of parents and others, that the new approaches would leave many children entertained perhaps but unable to read and write are almost certainly false. Surveys conducted by the Department of Education and Science suggest that reading ability has risen dramatically since the war. There are those who dispute this and point out that you would expect low attainments from those whose education had been interupted by the war—but the rise seems to have been consistent ever since. The truth is that society makes very much greater demands on young people now than it did even 20 years ago. If there is failure, it is failure to meet a higher standard (except in copper-plate). What is more, many bright youngsters are not taking jobs they would have been glad to get in the past: they are going on maybe to higher education. This means that the quality of applicants for some jobs, especially very boring ones in offices, may be falling while the general quality of young school leavers is rising. Another measure may be examinations (which are discussed more fully in Chapter Eleven): more and more children today are reaching standards of attainment in secondary school examinations which were beyond all but the very few 20 years ago. But perhaps the most convincing evidence is the work of the children themselves. The doubters should at least allow themselves the pleasure of consulting the many anthologies now available, if not the schools themselves.

Mathematics

Most people are frightened by mathematics. They admit, with apology or defiance, that they are "no good at figures". We have all experienced a sense of vacant unreality stealing over us when a speaker or a television programme mentions too many percentages. We all distrust statistics, uneasily believing that "you can prove anything" with them—or that "there are lies, damned lies and statistics". When you come to think of it this is very odd. In the first place, mathematics has a very venerable place in the school curriculum. Arithmetic was there, with reading and writing, in the dame schools and in the first attempts at state initiative in education. So you would have thought that mathematics would have become as familiar and acceptable as English. What is more, most pupils and their parents regard mathematics as useful and necessary. There is every practical incentive to study and do well in it. Yet the mistrust remains.

We have to start by understanding the basis of this distrust, for two reasons. In the first place, there is a revolution going on in the teaching of mathematics in schools which is more swift and complete than the changes in any other subject—and this revolution has grown from dissatisfaction with previous methods and practices. There must be something wrong, many teachers argued, when a subject as long standing, familiar and important as mathematics was so universally hated and so largely ineffective. So the fact that you and I find ourselves floundering is one reason why the schools are trying to see that our children do not. But there is a second reason why our mistrust of mathematics needs to be faced: we already feel so insecure that we are in no position to understand, let alone welcome, the revolution in the schools. We suffer the disadvantage that with luck our children will escape: we feel beaten from the start. So there is a double barrier. Mathematics is something we almost instinctively shy away from anyway and the fact that it now looks quite different from what we ourselves remember is enough to kill any momentary interest.

Still, we need not despair. Let us have a look first, at the old familiar mathematics. It may turn out to be not quite so imposing after all. The most obvious thing about it was that it was very firmly subdivided into separate subjects: arithmetic, algebra, geometry, trigonometry. The syllabuses for these were normally quite distinct, and they were taught in different periods, often by different people, and there was rarely any suggestion of a connection between them. Many of us, of course, tackled only one branch— arithmetic. It was frequently assumed that only those who showed the greatest proficiency here could be expected to make anything of the others.

What characterised them all was a great reliance on rote learning, on the application of formulae, on the practice of examples. You learned the tricks and performed them continually. In arithmetic, the foundation was the multiplication tables which were chanted and tested daily. (In the eighteenth century children multiplied by reference to a simple ready-reckoner: it was the Victorians who insisted that the thing should be learned). Then came practice in the four processes of addition, subtraction, multiplication and division (long and short)—of numbers, fractions, decimals, money, weights and measures. To these were often added the mysteries of percentages and interest, simple and compound. In each case there was a formula— put down the three and carry one, bring down the next figure from the divisor and so on—and what you had to do was manipulate it. At the end of every chapter of a typical text book there were a couple of pages of identical exercises which you worked your way through. In algebra there was a similar manipulation of formulae: $(a + b)^2 = a^2 + 2ab + b^2$, simultaneous equations and the like. In geometry there were theorems (by Pythagoras and Apollonius and others) which were similarly learned and practised incessantly.

I have used the past tense throughout here, but there are still schools where this approach to mathematics survives, and there are still teachers who defend it. What they argue is that all this forms the basis of mathematics, which has to be mastered before anything more important or interesting can be attempted. This is a common view in education: that learning anything demands, first of all, a period of drudgery. Only later, in this view, can the pupil or student discover the real interest of the subject. Of course, every activity, in school as in life, involves a large element of routine, but what the old method quite clearly did was to put people off education for good. There is nothing dull about mathematics, at any stage, and there is no excuse for making it so. The fact is that one rarely needs the techniques so painfully acquired. How many people ever touch simultaneous equations or cosines after leaving school? And even the vaunted multiplication tables are more of a hindrance than a help: in later life what one normally needs to know is not that seven nines are sixty three, but that seven ninepences are five and threepence. (Perhaps with decimalization the tables will really come into their own!).

This remoteness from reality pervaded the old textbooks and the old methods. There is in some play or novel a scene where a schoolboy is struggling with the problem of the rate at which a bath would be filled if the water were running in at one speed and out at another—only to be met by his mother who thought that only a fool would *try* to fill a bath in those circumstances. I myself remember spending a year or two on trigonometry at school but only understood the point of it when we did navigation in the cadet force.

But this is not the only objection to the old mathematics.

Perhaps the oddest thing about it was that, so far from giving people a good grounding, it tried to do something which was too difficult too early. It was, after all, intensely abstract. It presented pupils with formulae and gave them practice in using them. But we now know how long it takes children to grasp the ideas behind these formulae and to think in abstract terms. In a very real sense, the old mathematics presented them with the most difficult parts first. What this meant was that very often children never mastered the formulae at all: they were remote and incomprehensible. Even worse, in some ways, was the fact that very many children learned them happily, manipulated them perfectly—and never understood what they were doing. To take a personal experience again, I got a perfectly good credit in the old general school certificate (the equivalent of O level) in mathematics. In a classroom test in which we had to do twenty five exercises on Pythagoras's theorem I completed the lot on the mistaken basis that the great geometer had shown that the square on the hypotenuse of a right angled triangle was equal to the product (instead of the sum) of the squares on the other two sides. Anyone who remembers any geometry at all will see that this mistake would have been impossible if I had understood a word of what I was doing. Fortunately for me that sort of ignorance was perfect for O level.

Learning mathematics in that way is like being given a message to deliver in a language you do not understand. You can, with application, memorise the message and repeat it faithfully whenever required. But it does not teach you anything, and if someone should respond to the message you are left in embarrassed speechlessness. For mathematics *is* a language, which enables you to say things you cannot say in any other way. It is a separate way of looking at things, of understanding and solving problems. This is what the old mathematics lacked above all. There it was a matter of learning the tricks and applying them to textbook questions. It did not offer an extra way of looking at, and tackling, all the problems of daily life.

Now, how does the new mathematics work out in

practice? I have said that you will find quite a lot of the old still in use in schools. Schools and teachers change gradually and you are likely to find the old and the new running alongside each other. Perhaps most schools will have begun to try to relate their mathematics to the needs and experience of their pupils. Even textbook problems will be about budgeting, fitting out a home, hire-purchase, travel and the like. This change can be even more significant than it looks. It may not seem much that academic problems of simple and compound interest should now lead young people to understand the significance of paying interest (in hire purchase) on the whole sum over the whole period of the loan: or that they can quickly work out the most economical way of carpeting a room. The point is that they will be thinking differently about everything in their daily lives, thinking more precisely, more accurately, more rationally.

Those schools which have taken the new mathematics furthest are trying to do more than this, to extend the creative abilities of their pupils, through mathematics. One of the greatest differences between the old ways and the new is the extent to which mathematics are now an imaginative enterprise and an aesthetic experience. And basic to this is the abolition of fear and distrust.

Perhaps this is the place to give an example of the kind of thing that is becoming increasingly common in secondary schools, and which parents have consistently found puzzling. We parents are used to counting in tens. When we were small we even used to write "hundreds, tens and units" over our sums. The chances are that man has done this because he has ten digits (eight fingers and two thumbs). When he counts he goes: one two three four five six seven eight nine ten—which he writes one-nought and continues one-one (eleven), one-two, one-three, and so on. But (to take a familiar example) supposing you were an octopus. Then you would have only eight tentacles and would presumably count: one two three four five six seven eight . . . Here you would run out of tentacles and so you would have to call eight "one-nought" and continue, one-one, one-two and so on. At one-seven you would pause: the next number would have to be two-nought. (Just as for men, counting in tens, the number after one-nine is two-nought). It is worth having a go at this in figures on a piece of paper, and you will find that it helps to say one-nought, one-one, one-two and later two-nought and so on, when you get into double figures, even though, when you are counting in tens you write: 1 2 3 4 5 6 7 8 9 10 11 12 13 . . . and when you are counting in eights you write: 1 2 3 4 5 6 7 10 11 12 13 14 15 16 17 20 21 22 23 24 25 26 27 30 31 . . . Try counting in some other number. Take four: 1 2 3 10 11 12 13 20 21 . . . Try six, or nine. The number that you are counting in is known as a "base", and it is written rather small behind the figure concerned: 2345₈ is 2345 in the base 8. You can of course add and subtract in different bases. In the base 10, 26 + 15 is 41. In the base 8, 38 + 63 is 123. Try some others—remembering that as with the familiar ten, when you get to the base number you write one-nought.

Now let us try with the base two. We are counting, here, in twos and units. So we start with one, but then we have already reached our base number (two) so we have to write in one-nought. Our next number is one-one—but then we are in the same situation that the base ten is in when it gets to ninety nine. We have to say one-nought-nought. Then one-nought-one, one-one-nought, one-one-one, and so on. Try it in figures: 1 10 11 100 101 110 111 1000 1001 1010 1011 1100 1101 1110 1111 10000 . . . If this is a little too like science fiction, remember the old weights granny used to have in the kitchen. There was an ounce weight, a two-ounce one, a four-ounce (¼ lb.), and eight-ounce (½ lb.) and a sixteen-ounce (1 lb.). Let us put them in order on the right of the page. On the left we can write the amounts that we want to weigh, and in the appropriate columns we can put the numbers of the weights of each size we shall need. (I got this explanation at a talk given by one of Her Majesty's Inspectors: I only hope the enlightenment of that audience will be matched for the readers of this book)

To weigh, we need	16	8	4	2	1 oz. wts.
one ounce					1
two ounces				1	0
three ounces				1	1
four ounces			1	0	0
five ounces			1	0	1
six ounces			1	1	0
seven ounces			1	1	1
eight ounces		1	0	0	0
ten ounces		1	0	1	0
thirteen ounces		1	1	0	1
sixteen ounces	1	0	0	0	0

You can work the others out for yourself. In any case, you can compare them with those above. Perhaps the base two is not so bothersome as it once seemed.

This "binary system" (base two) is significant because it is made to order for computers. A computer can only use two symbols, because a switch has two positions—on and off—corresponding to 1 and 0. Any number can be expressed in this way—though of course the expression gets gigantically long. Fortunately computers are built not to mind that.

But the point of the base two and all the other bases is not that children can pretend to be computers. It is that their attitude to numbers entirely changes. I wonder if you have been able to get an idea of this from the examples given earlier. A child who is used to counting in different bases is not likely to be intimidated by numbers. He feels he is the boss: that he can make numbers do what he wants them to do. Those of us whose mathematical education has left us worried and suspicious may envy the new confidence and ability.

Perhaps we are now ready to look inside a modern mathematical text book. The first thing that may surprise us is that there is no obvious distinction, along the old lines, between arithmetic, algebra, geometry and so on. One page may remind us of geometry, another of algebra, another of arithmetic—while others may be full of all kinds of unfamiliar signs and symbols. The second thing we shall notice is that probably every page is filled with pictures and diagrams. All the time, the book will be trying to make visible the abstract ideas in which mathematics deals. The third difference comes at the end of each page. Instead of a page or two of exercises, all worked on the same principles, giving little more than routine practice, there will be problems which the child will have to think about from scratch. In many ways the exercises will closely resemble the text itself. There is much less isolated explanation followed by repeated practice. The facts and principles of mathematics are conveyed by getting the children themselves to discover what they are. The line between instruction and practice is scarcely visible.

CHAPTER SIX

Science and technology

In the grammar schools of the past, science was quite a distinctive activity. It took place, for a start, in rooms perhaps twice the normal size, which were fitted out not with desks but with long, broad, high benches, with sinks and gas taps for Bunsen burners, at which one sat on high ascetic stools. The general atmosphere was derelict and smelly. I myself remember a much loved physics master, who was also a sorely tried deputy head. For many physics lessons he would enter the door at the back of the long laboratory, puff slowly towards the front saying "Take out your rough books and put down today's date." He would then leave by the door at the front of the room, never to reappear again that lesson. When he stayed with us, we were engaged in a number of "experiments". I remember discovering "the thermal capacity of a copper calorimeter" which was a matter largely of boiling water in a can. We also sprinkled iron filings over magnets in the manner of those toys now widely sold for five-year olds. This, it appeared, was physics. There were also chemistry and biology. These were entirely distinct subjects, having only the method of instruction in common. Either the pupils would follow in groups some chemical or physical process to its foregone conclusion or there would be a demonstration, more or less explosive as the case may be, at the master's bench. After this, we would copy down an account of the "experiment" either from the board or from dictation.

This description is of what was generally available to those fortunate children in grammar schools and other schools which had laboratories. For most children science got little further than "nature study" in which the pupils identified and drew twigs, leaves and the outlines of trees.

That it is not an exaggeration can be seen from glancing through many of the official reports on science teaching. They complain of syllabuses without a pattern or thread, so pupils cannot see the drift and purpose of what they are doing and neither acquire an organized and usable body of knowledge and experience, nor come to understand the characteristics of a scientific attitude. What is more, it is very hard for pupils, or indeed anyone else, to see the significance of what they meet in the school laboratory for life in the world outside.

These weaknesses in the teaching of science must be held at least partly responsible for the general suspicion of science among school children. After all, science has provided some of the most exciting or terrifying moments in human history. It must for example have been a bit of a shock to understand that the earth was not flat. Nuclear explosions are scarcely dull. To understand the secret of life is hardly pedestrian. There can be few things more relevant to daily life than the study of electricity, radio waves, or machines. And yet the traditional view of school science is that it is boring and irrelevant.

The purpose of new methods in science teaching is twofold. The first is to give children the methods of science as a tool in meeting the demands of life. Of course, there can be plenty of debate about what constitutes scientific method. One robust scientist held that scientific method was anything that worked. In this view what is common to all science is commonsense. But this is being unfairly simple minded. It is true that the raw materials of science are those which can be discovered by using our senses—even if we have to extend these with devices like microscopes or telescopes. But there is more to science than observation. We need explanations too. And perhaps for most people a scientist is a man who studies a whole lot of things until he discovers something. This is not quite what science is about, and it is less boring and more creative than most people think. What a scientist does is to come up with an explanation and then to check it. For example in the early 19th century astronomers noticed that there was a "wobble" in the orbit of the planet Uranus, and a couple of them suggested that this was due to the effect of gravitation from another, unknown, planet. They even worked out where that planet "ought" to be, and when someone was able to train upon that part of the sky a sufficiently powerful telescope, they found it sure enough. This is a very much more typical example of scientific behaviour. Of course, scientists tend to know a good deal before they start thinking and guessing. But often great strides are made because someone has an idea—a hypothesis—which he then checks. Of course, what distinguishes science from other feats of the human imagination is precisely the checking by observation. What you have to do with a scientific hypothesis is to decide what would prove it false. For example, the hypothesis that the planet Neptune existed in a particular position could be shown to be false if the planet did not appear there. But scientific method is not only a question of discovery; it is a way of thinking.

There is room for only one illustration of this. At the heart of science is the principle that statements of fact should be based upon observation, not on unsupported authority: or as one of the founders of scientific method put it, the determination "never to accept as true what I did not know to be *evidently* so". This seems fairly obvious, put like that, and most people do not realise how very recently it has been generally accepted or how few peoples in the world have accepted it yet. Through most of history men have respected authority and tradition more than observation. A lot of people still believe things that have no basis except in tradition and hearsay. Here are some examples: ostriches eat nails; repeated exercise in childhood has a permanent effect on the growth of the muscles; hanging a dozen men every year uniquely helps to prevent murders; getting your feet wet gives you a cold; immigrants are a burden on the social services (the reverse of this is true); you can tell what will happen to you next week by referring to your date of birth: the resurrection of the body and the life everlasting. This sort of belief has always been normal throughout history in large matters as in small.

What a scientific education does is to make them questionable. It enables children to be sceptical of authority and ready to check what they are told. It encourages the rational discussion of great issues and the swift determination of small ones. Scientific method is not only a kind of vocational training for scientists. It is a weapon with which young people can meet the promises of political parties, the precepts of parents, the blandishments of advertisers, the claims of group loyalty, solidarity, patriotism—and all the bombarding assertions with which they are constantly assailed.

The second purpose of the new methods in science teaching is to relate the subject matter of science to the lives and interests of the pupils. This does not mean that the subject matter is limited by the pupils' experience; but it means that science teachers today start from that experience and lead them to discoveries in ideas and worlds they had never dreamt of. Very often this is done by taking a large major theme or group of themes on which the work is concentrated. For example, a teacher might decide to make the biology of man a central point of reference. This is a gigantic study in itself, involving the structure and function of the body and its various parts and organs: the human life cycle from conception to death, together with the principles of growth and development; the mechanism of heredity; health and hygiene; the senses and the science of behaviour and learning: man in his environment in the past, present and future, and in various parts of the world. Much of this study would be recognizably the traditional biology, though it would probably be less coy and more scientific about most of the human bodily functions. There might be rather less emphasis on flowers and amoebas and rather more on people. But this syllabus offers very much more than the old biology course. It brings in chemistry, psychology, sociology, anthropology. And it is all of central interest to young people. Few topics fascinate people more than the way their own bodies work—witness the medical advice columns in all those papers and magazines. It is also of central importance to young people: almost every topic listed earlier is directly useful and necessary in everyday life.

But the biology of man may be only the central core of studies in science. A teacher might lead out from it to the study of all living things: he might try to show the nature and variety of life, the way in which man, animals and plants are all interdependent; he might encourage a respect for living things and the conservation of wild life and the countryside; he might show the application of biology to agriculture and its contribution to feeding humanity. Another lead might take the class into an understanding of the continuity of life, through the theory of evolution and its supporting evidence. Yet another might introduce man's whole environment, the earth and its place in the universe. A class might start from man's physical limitations to understand his use of machines and engines, learning about the sources, forms and measurement of energy; or from the limitations of the senses to discover about light and sound and all kinds of communications. Another study might investigate the nature, development and uses of material, ideas about the structure of elements and compounds. In all this, the "subjects" studied, in the old fashioned sense, include chemistry, physics, astronomy, mathematics, mechanics, geology: the list is almost endless. But they are not presented as arbitrary subjects any more, without reference either to other studies or to life itself. Neither do they remain stuck within the children's own narrow range of immediate interest. They grow from that interest and remain relevant to it but lead to a creative exploration beyond.

In a very few schools, the study of energy, materials and machines has begun to be pursued in an applied context. Science has become technology. There are a number of reasons for this tentative development. The first is that the structure of employment is changing, making many more jobs in the professional and the middle levels, and many fewer in manual occupations. This has given rise to continuing fears that the nation may face a shortage of engineers. (This fear, if not groundless, at least has no

CHAPTER SIX

visible ground.) The second reason is that people increasingly feel that in a society where complicated machines are common, all children should have some familiarity with machinery. The third is that a technological education is a valid and necessary kind of education.

This last view often strikes people as odd. They seem to think that technological and technical studies may be all right for people who like messing about with oily rags or who are, in the dismissive phrase, "good with their hands", but cannot hold the interest of intelligent people. What is really odd is that people do think like this, especially in a country where the imagination, inventiveness and creativity of engineers made the industrial revolution which produced our modern society. Technology is what distinguishes the modern age from all those which preceded it. The achievement of the Victorian railway builders, in aesthetic as well as engineering terms, was as great as that of the medieval cathedral builders. An aeroplane is, among other things, a work of art. (My own personal view is that one reason why modern art is in a mess is that science and technology are absorbing so much creative imagination.)

Why, then, has technology such a dim reputation? One explanation may be its historical association with dirt. Another may be a permanent misunderstanding, among teachers and pupils alike, of what an engineer does. Attitudes are only slowly changing, but it is quite certain that, as time goes on, the science laboratories and workshops of the new secondary schools will grow more alike, the application of science will accompany its understanding —and more schools will offer (as one does now) prizes for such projects as the design and building of a model bridge capable of carrying the greatest load. I least, I hope so.

CHAPTER SEVEN

Modern languages

In the past, the learning of a foreign language was considered one of the hall marks of a secondary education. Indeed, people felt that without it a child could not be said to have had a secondary education at all. But, even today, half of the children of Britain are uneducated in this sense. They never get a chance to start learning a foreign language. Of those who do start, very many give up after a year or two. One of the reasons why the country is re-organizing its secondary education is so that more children might start and persevere.

There are perhaps four reasons why learning another language is important. The first is entirely utilitarian. More people than ever are travelling abroad. Their education should at least have given them the capacity to get about, to order meals or accommodation, to strike up a conversation with people they meet. It is too great a handicap for British children if they cannot do these simple things outside their own country. Perhaps many people might regard this as no more than a passing annoyance, but even they might see that successful exporting could depend in part upon a firm's having staff who can make themselves understood abroad, and although moves towards political union in Europe seem halting and half-hearted, there seems little doubt that people will increasingly need to be at home in other languages.

Most people can probably be persuaded of the usefulness of modern languages, even though they doubt whether everybody needs them equally. But there are other reasons for introducing them to children. Language is the key to a culture. Of course it is entirely possible to read the literature of other countries in translation—and there have never before been so many excellent translations in cheap paper-back editions. But everybody who has been able to read a book in its original language knows that something is lost in translation. A serious argument for learning French, German—and even Latin—is that there are so many books written in these languages. A side effect of learning another language is a better understanding of one's own. It may sound odd, but many teachers have noticed that when children start learning a foreign language their English improves. The reason presumably is that the new language gives them an incentive to think about words, to look at what they themselves are saying with a fresh eye and to take more notice of what they have done almost naturally or instinctively. As the poet said, "What do they know of England, who only England know?". The same is true of English.

In the past language teaching suffered from a desire to make it academic. The first thing children learnt was how to "conjugate" the verb "to be" or "to have": je suis, tu es, il est, nous sommes, vous êtes, ils sont. Gradually a great stock of such conjugations was learnt by heart, and learning a language was a matter of applying these remembered runes to a phrase or sentence conceived in English. It meant that children were not so much speaking French as constantly translating from English into French. It is likely that the process went back to the teaching of Latin and ancient Greek. These languages are no longer spoken, and scholars had created for both of them an elaborate grammar to explain the ways in which they had been written. It was thought that the best way of learning the language was to learn the grammar. To do the classicists justice, a movement against this form of teaching started among them early in the century, when a number of teachers used what they called the "direct method" in which the language was first of all spoken and written and only later explained in terms of grammar. There was always something rather artificial about this in the case of Latin, because nobody actually speaks it now. But its application to the teaching of modern languages is obvious.

What a modern language teacher tries to do is to encourage fluency. Children learn quickly how to use a language in speech first and then in writing. It is only at a much later stage that grammar is introduced. Come to think of it, this is how English children learn English. It is only after they have a good grasp of the language, that anybody bothers with grammar, and as we have seen, fewer and fewer teachers now regard grammar as anything but an interesting addition.

One of the consequences of this change in attitude is that many more children are capable of tackling languages. In the past the emphasis on grammar was so off-putting that many children failed to cope at all. Even the children of known ability, in grammar schools, found themselves spending five years getting a language to O level standard— only to find themselves tongue-timed and embarrassed when faced with a cafe proprietor in Boulogne. It seemed as if French must be fantastically difficult if five years of study by a bright child led to this sort of incompetence. The truth was of course that the children had spent five years on quite unnecessary things, and had spent very little time actually learning how to use French. Teachers have discovered, what they might have guessed, that if you concentrate on teaching the language for use, there is almost no child who cannot succeed in it to some extent.

In one of the very first comprehensive schools in Britain, a large school for girls, the senior modern language mistress (who had come from a grammar school) consciously sought to extend the study of modern languages to as many of the girls as possible. But she felt that it would be unfair to face the least able girls with what he felt would be a difficulty they were not likely to overcome. All the streams in the first year, except two, were offered a foreign languages. In the event, the girls in these two streams were bewildered and angry about it. They demanded to know why they had been left out, and the head of modern languages found her explanations rang hollow and unconvincing. The girls were introduced to Italian (which is much easier in the early stages than French or German) and were taught through the direct method. It turned out that they were quite able to master simple conversation, to read and write with some confidence, to enter into the thought and life of another country—and their English improved. At least this linguist has never since made the mistake of assuming that some children are incapable of learning a foreign language.

The new methods, of course, involve new teaching techniques. Most obvious among these are visits to countries abroad, and most of the others are classroom substitutes for such visits. They include films and film strips, television, radio, record players and tape recorders. A modern language teacher is likely to have a whole battery of these mechanical aids in the classroom. Perhaps one in ten schools has what is called a language laboratory. This is in effect a special two-channel form of tape recorder. Each pupil sits in a sound-proof booth with the equipment in front of him and a pair of headphones on. He listens to the master track, which is under the control of the teacher: he cannot rub it off accidentally or on purpose. The other track is under his own control: he can record his responses, check them with the model or instructions of the master track, rub off his own efforts and try again until he is satisfied. While he is doing this, the teacher is sitting at a "console" or control post, and he can listen in to what any student is doing and intervene if necessary with help or guidance. What the language laboratory means is that every student can be working on his own, at his own pace, all the time. In an ordinary classroom, after all, only one pupil can answer any one question at a time. The booth and the headphones may give a pupil a sense of seclusion and even the shyest pupil can practise without self-consciousness or fear of ridicule. What is more, the teacher can focus his attention on any one pupil without interrupting the work of others.

On the other hand, the language laboratory can be impersonal. It cannot converse, it has no spontaneity. It can be no substitute for human contact and the practice of a conversation. What is more, if it is sloppily used, it can encourage children in errors quite as well as in accuracy, and like all mechanical things, it tends to break down. Most teachers who use a language laboratory claim it is a help, but there is probably not enough evidence yet to decide whether it is essential.

The most popular modern language in secondary schools is still French, France is after all the nearest foreign country, and French is still spoken in large parts of the world. The second most popular, though a long way behind, is German and the third Spanish. Italian and Russian are growing more common. A few schools offer Chinese. What is slightly surprising is that probably more children still learn Latin than learn German, at any rate for a full secondary course.

CHAPTER EIGHT

Social studies

One of the problems for parents trying to understand what their children are doing at school is that the names for things keep changing. PT becomes PE (see Chapter Nine) and so on. So parents may be puzzled to see a new subject called Social Studies cropping up in the timetable. They need not worry unduly: the sum of human knowledge does not change all that quickly, and they can assume that under cover of social studies much may be going on which would be familiar by another name. This assumption may be confirmed as they fail to find old favourites like history and geography with separate places in the timetable.

But the change is more than one of name. As we have seen in all these chapters on the content of school courses, the trend is away from treating school subjects in isolation from each other. Teachers are trying, more and more, to show the relevance of one subject for another, and this can be true even where subjects are not formally grouped together. Such a grouping has other advantages: new and unfamiliar subjects can be accommodated within the total framework. Social studies is a case in point. There is an important sense in which geography and history complement each other, and their insights can be extended by subjects which are relatively new to schools, like sociology, economics, psychology and anthropology. All this can be accommodated under social studies.

Let us start with the more familiar subjects. History has always been in all but the most rudimentary school timetables for many reasons. It seems to fill a basic human need: even pretty primitive human societies have stories which purport to show the origins of the race or tribe. Many of these we regard as legendary—like the direct descent of Greek or Anglo-Saxon heroes from gods. The social need to establish origins is like the personal need to know one's own parents and grandparents. There is something deeply satisfactory, almost peaceful, even to irreligious people, about an assertion like: "In the beginning, God created the heaven and the earth." And, to some people's surprise, a similar feeling is satisfied by the theory of evolution. Men need to know where they came from and by what steps.

A society is held together by the things its members have in common. Its history is one of the most obvious of these, along with culture and customs. So history is important as a unifier: it helps to make British children feel British, Europeans feel European—and could, if properly taught, help to make mankind feel like one race.

But history does more than this. It is, after all, about men and women in different ages and places coping with problems of organization, Government, revolution, even survival. It is about human achievement and the inter-action between men and societies. At one time it was taught as if the lives of great men offered a series of examples to be emulated by the young. Today's attitude is somewhat more critical: it invites children to understand rather than to admire. Others have sought to claim that a study of history offers direct lessons for today's affairs: "history repeats itself" is a familiar slogan. But men are quite as likely to be misled by history as enlightened. Sir Anthony Eden thought, when he invaded Egypt, that he was again fighting Hitler: but the circumstances were different and the mistake costly. What history shows is men reacting in many ways to many different circumstances. It holds general, not particular, lessons. But a study of it can increase understanding—of how and why people act as they do, of the limitations of policy, of the possibility of change. Some of these lessons are more easily learned by reference to the past. A knowledge of how King John travelled the country from one of his castles to another, to draw on their treasuries, may give a more vivid feeling for the dependence of policy upon available resources than the complications of a

modern Finance Bill; the wars and intrigues of the Renaissance princes of Italy may offer the most colourful guide
to the maxim that in politics you have to foresee and allow
for *all* the consequences of your actions; the blindness of
nineteenth century British governments to the possibility
of mitigating the Irish famine, may powerfully suggest that
many modern evils are more avoidable than they look;
a short course in the consequences of revolutions from
ancient times to the present day might inhibit some of the
wilder student claims for revolution now.

In all this the study of history offers an exercise in
imaginative understanding. In this sense it can be thought
of as an art. But history is also a science, with rigorous
standards of evidence. Most of what I have been discussing
earlier could arise quite as well from myth and legend as
from history, indeed has done so until quite recently.
History today asks additional questions: is it true? what
really happened? So a study of history has this extra purpose and lesson, to study the sources of the information we
have, to decide whether they are reliable, to compare one
with another. The sources are extremely varied: some are
written, others are under the ground and have to be dug
up by archeologists. Imagination and speculation about
the past, checked against the evidence, is the basis of
historical study.

There is a sense in which human geography can be
thought of almost as history in the present. Stone age
peoples still exist. Most societies in the world are pre-
scientific. Americans live in our future, just as peoples in
mostly agricultural countries are living in our past. But
geography is also about the earth, so to speak, before men
got at it. It is about the structure of the land, the move-
ments of the oceans, about climate, natural vegetation and
mineral and other resources. It shows how man has
manipulated these but is still dependent upon them, in
agriculture and industry.

It is becoming increasingly common for geography and
history to be tackled as a single subject, covering human life,
behaviour and achievement. But teachers who do this very

often find themselves broadening the course still further. Many, for example, cannot see that history should stop at some arbitrary date, like 1945. The world then was quite different from that of young people today: it was still largely ruled by empires, for example. But young people now at school have no experience of empires in the old sense. Most colonies became free before many of today's secondary school children had learned to read. So, under the title of social studies, history and geography became current affairs, embracing modern forms of government, politics, international relations. But these modern studies involve new disciplines too: economics, sociology and psychology are increasingly finding their way into the curriculum. All have special insights to offer. Economics, for example, is the science of industrialisation, and it is hard to understand modern industrial societies without some knowledge of it. But some of its concepts are relevant to daily life, are also homely. Take, for instance, the concept of the margin, by which economists mean the "extra". This leads to such questions as this: is the extra effort (or cost) of doing something justified by the extra benefit or gain? Many daily decisions are of this kind, though perhaps most people do not realise it and decide badly as a consequence. A shop offers two articles—washing machines, say, or cars—one rather dearer than the other. Do we always ask ourselves quite clearly whether the extra gadgets (or other advantages) are worth the *extra* cost? It is odd that we do not, because we have at least proverbially understood that the extra risk of breaking the camel's back is not worth the extra straw.

A lot of the insights of history are made explicit in a study of psychology. This is the science of human behaviour: it investigates it, classifies, theorises and checks the theories. Of course it can be fun to apply these psychological theories to the lives of historical figures: how far, for example, was Churchill's success during the war due to his suddenly finding himself doing in reality what he had always done in his own fantasy world? But for young people the insights of psychology can be most relevant to helping them to understand and cope with their own situation. For example, a boy may find after leaving school that he has difficulty in getting on with his immediate boss. Such a situation may make life a misery all round, may indeed lead to his leaving this job, only to find the same difficulty in another. An acquaintanceship with psychology can help to make it clear to him whether the causes of his difficulty lie mostly within himself or with his boss. Is it that he has himself been unable to come to terms with his own father, and thus resents and mistrusts all authority? Or is it that the boss feels inadequate, frustrated or insecure and is "taking it out" on the boy? Young people are fascinated by human relationships and can benefit directly from an introduction to a systematic study of them.

Sociology is also about human behaviour, but this time about the behaviour of people in groups. To take the most obvious example, it includes the study of the family. Families are differently organized in different societies. In many of them the word implies much more than the mother, father and two or three children that we have become used to in England. It means the whole complex of parents and children, grandparents, aunts, uncles, nephews, nieces, cousins—and wives. The three-bedroomed house, so common in Britain, would not be regarded in most other parts of the world as at all suitable for a "family". Differences in family customs mean different ways of bringing up children. In Western societies children grow gradually to be independent. They are encouraged to "stand on their own feet" and take their own decisions as adults. In Eastern societies, the most important decision, the choice of a husband or wife, is taken, not by the individual, but by the family. What the study of sociology does is to show the importance of social institutions, like the family. It can help young people to see that social arrangements are not somehow innate or unalterable: customs differ from place to place. And it can show them very clearly what sort of society they live in, its limitations and opportunities.

The purpose of all social studies is to give children an understanding of man, and in particular man as a "social animal." This may be done by studying an immediate neighbourhood or town, or a continent or empire. It may be achieved through the past or the present, through the familiar or the exotic. It may involve long-standing disciplines like history or geography—or new ones, like sociology, which are being introduced only now into a very few schools. All these are ways of giving children and young people a sympathetic understanding of their human condition.

CHAPTER NINE

Skill and imagination

There was a time when it was implied that practical skills were some sort of compensation for the less academic children. A sense of failure in English and mathematics, in this view, might be mitigated by success in handicraft. The football field was the preserve of the "muddied oaf." This has been one of the drearier consequences of the dominance of self-styled academic education. What more and more people are coming to realise is that the sort of intelligence which is measured by intelligence tests and the sort of memory which is needed for most academic examinations are not the only qualities which education should nourish or the only grounds for achievement and happiness in life. Qualities of creativeness, sensitivity, imagination, physical skill, perseverence, judgment, are at least as important as a high score in an intelligence test or O level. Indeed one educator has gone so far as to say that what most tests reveal is an ability to solve relatively trivial problems with accuracy and speed, whereas what life demands is the ability to tackle important problems slowly and to learn from one's mistakes. Along with this dawning realisation that intelligence is not everything (though we must not fall into the opposite trap of supposing it is nothing) is the realisation of the extent to which physical and practical activities make demands on intellect and character, not on "mere" physical agility. It is for these reasons that this chapter covers what may seem to some parents to be rather odd contrasts: music and physical education, home economics and art, and so on. The ancient Greeks, who have been the accepted model for English academic education, except in practice, would have entirely under-

The purpose of this selection of photographs is to show
something of the range and variety of the work to which
an effective comprehensive school can attain.

These pictures were all taken in one school, and this is
in no way a balanced presentation of what goes on in
secondary schools; there is also a good deal of reading,
writing and listening to teachers that must go on in any
school, no matter how it is organised.

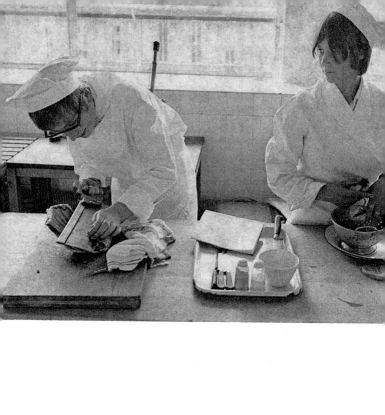

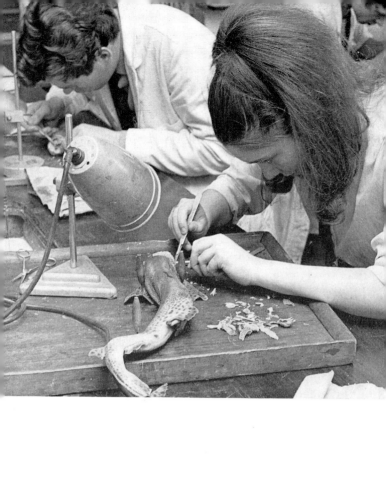

stood these (to us) strange alliances. They assumed that music and physical education drama and art were all part of the same thing—religion!

Another reason for bringing these subjects together is that they are all ones in which the pupils are executants. In music they may get no further than singing (though many are now learning musical instruments), in physical education they may barely stagger up the wall-bars, in woodwork they may make nothing more complicated than a toothbrush holder. Equally, as we have seen, the movement in all areas of study in the new secondary schools is towards pupils' taking more responsibility for their own work, being active rather than passive in class. Nevertheless, you can scarcely think of being passive in PE, music or handicraft lessons: all these are participant activities or they are nothing. They are what the Robbins committee called "executive" subjects. They are things you do.

And they are especially important in secondary education because pupils are all the more ready for them. Of course, the primary schools are famous for their art, PE and so on: there is no sudden flowering in the secondary schools. Indeed the secondary schools may still have a lot to learn in these fields. But the fact is that as children get older, and particularly as they become adolescent, their physical skills increase. It is not just that they grow stronger and have much greater endurance. They can also work to finer limits of detail. This is why secondary schools have, on the whole, more extensive playing fields and specialist workshops and studios.

Physical education is normally offered in two guises; lessons which are called "PE" and in games periods. The "gym" is a fairly familiar part of most schools. Even a Victorian barrack of a school may be expected to have wall-bars and apparatus in the hall for PE lessons. The emphasis these days is very much less on formal "drill" and very much more on the intelligent use of exercise and apparatus. The principles of gymnastics (as seen in Olympic Games) are becoming better understood to involve the service of strength and intelligence to grace of movement. Indeed the freedom and individuality which are coming to be common throughout secondary education, were introduced early into PE, through the new thinking in the specialist colleges.

Games often occupy an afternoon a week for each child in the school. The traditional games are football or hockey in winter and cricket, and athletics and netball in summer and these probably persist as the staple games. They were approved of in the past not only for providing exercise but also for promoting collaboration in competition. A team game also requires a common strategy and tactics. All these virtues remain.

But many PE and games teachers argue that neither formal PE nor organized games provide the answer for all children. They may not be a source of pleasure or self esteem for most pupils—who do not get into representative teams or who find themselves less than agile as they get older. These teachers are therefore trying to offer many more forms of exercise. Swimming is increasingly common. Modern and country dancing often attract girls who baulk at any other form of PE. Individual athletics may appeal to those for whom team games are anathema. So may sports involving individual or pairs of players: tennis, badminton, archery, fencing and judo. There seems to be no limit to the ingenuity of some schools. And, sad to say, many schools need it: there are still very many schools with inadequate gymnasia and playing fields or none at all.

It is not too fanciful to see that art and crafts also offer a physical education, in the sense that they depend upon and train physical skill, often to a very fine precision. Painting and drawing, modelling and pottery, carving, fabric printing, weaving, bookmaking and leather work all demand physical control. But art represents more than physical education: it can be an emotional, aesthetic and imaginative education too.

Art seems to have been one of man's earliest achievements. Even the miserable creatures living in caves, contending for a living against mammoths and sabre toothed tigers, drew on the cave walls. Art has to do with decoration and, less obviously, perhaps, with magic. It is no coincidence that some ancient peoples (and through them some modern ones too) had rules against making graven images. There is a very primitive sense, which perhaps the cavemen had, that to depict something was to have mastery over it. Certainly artists have painted and sculpted in order to gain understanding. Art has also to do with communication. Words are not the only means of expression open to us, and for somethings they are not even the best.

Some parents may feel all this is a little high flown, when we are talking about the artistic efforts of teenagers. But one has to show from the start that art and craft are not "frills" tacked on to the edge of proper education: they meet a fundamental human need. What is more, if well introduced in schools, painting, modelling and carving can be an emotional outlet for young people, a way of exploring feelings which they have kept suppressed in day to day life. They can be a way of reliving experience and of imagining anew. As one official report put it, in the arts young people can deal imaginatively with the real, and realistically with what is imagined. Art, in short, can help young people to come to terms with the world around them.

The results of this can be puzzling. Parents may feel that they are all too reminiscent of the whole modern movement in the arts: barbaric and incomprehensible. This need not surprise us. The important thing to remember is that neither modern art nor the productions of our own children are entirely random. We can try to be sympathetic even when we do not understand.

Art in school does not stop here, however. In painting and drawing there may still be a good deal of what parents would recognise as old fashioned skill. There may be that much less routine still-life in today's art rooms, but the training of observation, selection, accuracy and skill are still part of art lessons. It is spilling over, too, into what might be called "design." Pupils are encouraged to judge the goods and materials around them, to educate their own taste, to design their own clothes or furniture. It may even be, in a generation or two, that a British people will emerge who will not put up with the dreary mediocrity and down-right ugliness of much of urban living.

This capacity for creative design can emerge even more fully in handicraft. All of us can understand the satisfaction of making something for ourselves. The do-it-yourself movement testifies to it. Parents who enter a school on an open day or some other occasion can see the results of this enthusiasm in a classroom or workshop. The ambition of some of it may surprise them. The exhibits may include elegant and useful pottery, figures and heads modelled in clay or wood, chairs and tables, working models of machines, chic and well made clothes, simple precision tools and so on. (In making some of these the children may have had the use of machine tools). The usefulness of many of these achievements is not in question: skills well learned can serve in adult life. But usefulness is not the only motive for them. The chance to create, to make something from the beginning to one's own design, does not come all that often in the course of modern life. That it is available to young people is one of the continuing contributions of the schools. The contribution would be even more effective, no doubt, if the schools were better equipped. Many have art and handicraft rooms or workshops which may be the envy of the parents. But there are still a number which are able to offer only a very limited range of crafts, and in some accommodation for these is very poor or absent altogether.

Probably the worst provided for of all the executant and imaginative subjects is music. It may get only one period a week in the early years and is the subject most commonly dropped thereafter. It is the worst equipped and accom-modated subject, and there is a serious shortage of qualified teachers for it. Perhaps all these difficulties account for the paradox that the "pop" culture to which the children belong is heavily dominated by music while something like four in ten children at school regard music as useless and boring.

There is some evidence that this dismal picture is changing. Specific accommodation for music is being provided in new school buildings. Schools are beginning to equip orchestras with instruments, often with the help of an active parents' association. More important, music teachers are beginning to learn how to work with the "pop" music phenomenon rather than against it. Where these changes have been successful the musical life of a school can be very imposing, flourishing often after school hours more than it does in the formal timetable. Quite dramatic results can be gained in what seems an impossibly short time. The arrival of a new young music teacher may see a school orchestra and choir founded within a year and a public concert put on shortly after. The pupils may not only play and sing, but write music too. Properly conceived, music in schools can not only open to pupils the musical heritage of the world. It can also give them a greater understanding, appreciation and enjoyment of the pop culture which surrounds them.

Parents who find the jump from pop culture to domestic science (housecraft or home economics) too abrupt may be a little out of touch with their children's world. The young see no incompatibility. There will also be those who wonder how domestic science (whatever it is now called) comes to be in the same group of topics as art or music. I make no apology. Making a home, bearing and bringing up children, are quite the most creative things human beings ever do. Together they have characteristics of both an art and a science. They demand intelligence, imagination and practical skill.

And what most people have not realised is that for many children now at school, and perhaps for most, the drudgery will be taken out of it. Washing machines are increasingly general. Refrigerators will decimate shopping hours. Washing-up machines will be as common as television in ten years time. Of course, there will still be a lot to do in running a home. In some ways it will be more complicated. But for the first time in Britain it will soon be possible to regard marriage, home and children as more of a creative activity than a chore. Except in the farming out of children to wet nurses and nannies, the average Englishwoman is about to experience the command of servants (machines) known only to the upper classes of the past.

Some of this revolution is already reflected in the home economics rooms in schools. There are the banks of cookers and sinks of the familiar domestic science course, and there are the equally well known needlework rooms. But the change of name to "home economics" is not just arbitrary. It underlines the fact that the most difficult part of home making is not so much the cooking and cleaning as the management of what is really a very complex task. So in many schools now there is a school flat, in which pupils gain the concentrated experience of running a house for a week or more. Some times this is done with considerable realism. The flat is lived in, as far as possible, by the girls. Children from a nearby infant school have been known to be brought in to be fed and dressed, read to and entertained. Distractions and appointments are contrived, and so on.

Those who think that "management" is too high falutin a word to use about housewives, might care to remember how much the job is a matter of judgment and design, of choice and decision. The schools give help with this too, with courses on diet, dress, consumer products and value for money. Some include serious courses on the care of babies and young children. One ought to add (for frightened fathers) that cooking is not ignored.

There is still a long way to go before all schools offer an up to date home economics course: too many still concentrate on embroidery. And we are still a long way from the most crying need: home economics for boys.

CHAPTER TEN

Religious education

Religious education is the one great anomaly in British schools. It is the only subject which schools are compelled to offer by law. There is no law which says that all schools must offer English, mathematics, science or history, but there is one which says that "religious instruction shall be given" in all state schools. This instruction is to be in accordance with an agreed syllabus drawn up by a committee of representatives of the local authority, the teachers and the denominations. Every school day has also, by law, to begin with a single collective act of worship.

The origins of this anomaly go back a long way. It is enough to say here that it is now part of the law because of the complicated horse-trading that went on before and during the passing of the Education Act 1944. One of the difficulties of the time was to persuade the Churches to let their schools become part of an efficient national education service. Religion all round was part of the bargain.

It is not the law that individual children are compelled to have religious instruction, nor that individual teachers are compelled to give it. There are conscience clauses enabling parents to withdraw their children from both instruction and worship and for teachers to claim exemption from giving it. It is likely, however, that a number of parents and teachers do not press their rights here, so as not to embarrass either the children or the school.

The arguments for these legal provisions are, of course, Christian ones. Christians believe that religious education and the act of worship should influence the whole curriculum and set the tone of living and learning for the whole school. The act of worship, they believe, helps children to find a religious expression of their school lives and both illuminates personal relationships and introduces them to spiritual experience. Religious education, they similarly feel, teaches children to know and love God—which they regard as of central importance in life. There are probably very few Christians now (and most of them are Roman Catholic) who feel that not only Christianity but also the particular tenets of a single denomination should be taught to children. There seems to be a general desire to avoid involving children in religious controversy. On the other hand, there are probably a number of only vaguely Christian people who feel that facts about Christianity should be taught to children, whether or not children eventually believe in it, as being the best foundation for them ultimately to make up their own minds on the question. It is undeniable that Christianity has played a vital role in the history of Western societies.

Others feel that, leaving aside the particular beliefs of Christianity, there is a value in having lessons set aside for moral instruction. In the Education Act, 1944, the local authorities are, after all, meant to promote the moral development of the people.

It is probably fair to say that Christians have been giving a very great deal of thought to the special place of religious instruction in the school curriculum. They especially want parents to be fully aware of their rights to excuse their children from it and from the act of worship, and want proper arrangements made (as they rarely are) for those children excluded. They are also keen that the form of instruction and worship should be as inclusive as possible, so that children even of other faiths need not be withdrawn. In particular, many Christians are coming to believe that very much more needs to be known about what exactly it is that children understand when faced with specifically religious ideas and concepts. There is some anxiety that the spiritual development of children may not make it sensible to present to them much of the material which is now called religious education.

The absolute knock-down argument for religious

education, however, is that most parents seem to want it. Surveys suggest that more than three quarters of parents believe it should be given in schools and that probably the same proportion of teachers would volunteer to give it if asked.

The arguments against the special position of religious education are the reverse of those for. There are, of course, parents who believe that religion is mistaken or wicked. They make the point that because all schools have to offer it, they are precluded from choosing a non-religious school. Others object to the fact that "religious" in practice means Christian, because the syllabuses have been evolved in co-operation with the churches. In modern Britain other religions are becoming common, and it seems wrong to exclude at any rate in principle, Jews, Hindus, Muslims, Sikhs and so on. As we have seen, another strong objection comes from committed Christians who feel the law does more harm than good to Christianity. Their arguments rest on what is known about the way children develop: it seems fairly clear that children are not ready, until they reach adolescence, to understand religious ideas. What they grasp, in fact, is not what people assume they have been taught but an infantile version which turns them against Christianity for life.

The fact is, too, that the law is widely disregarded. Many teachers simply ignore the syllabuses. Some of them make the periods set aside for religious instruction indistinguishable from history, albeit of a rather limited kind. Others use the opportunity to have discussions about life, sex and morals. In many schools the single collective act of worship has also disappeared, being replaced either by one assembly a week, or by prayers in the classrooms. Perhaps in most schools, the specifically Christian or even religious aspects of the occasion have virtually disappeared: the singing is not confined to hymns, the readings are from books other than the Bible, the prayers have given way to headmaster's notices. Perhaps the most serious objection to the law is that there is no way of enforcing it when, as now, it is so commonly broken.

As for the question of moral instruction, the opponents of religious education by law argue that this need not be attached to a particular religious faith, and would be better if it were not. Then doubts about the faith need not lead to a rejection of the moral instruction. Some go further, and suggest that moral education comes better from example than from precept, and that a teacher's whole actions and attitudes, throughout the curriculum, are likely to be more influential than set lessons.

Most opponents of the present arrangements probably do not oppose Christian teaching as such: they may think it mistaken, but would not, as it were, want to legislate against its being taught (as is the case in the United States). They wish only to remove its special status. If most parents want it and most teachers would teach it, there seems little point in having a law to enforce it, especially since enforcement is impossible.

The question is likely to be a matter of permanent controversy, and individual schools will continue to meet the difficulties in their separate and often idiosyncratic ways.

CHAPTER ELEVEN

The new pattern of learning

In the last six chapters we have been looking at the curriculum of the new secondary schools. Of course, you are likely to come across ideas and methods like those discussed in any secondary school. No one kind of school has a monopoly of new ideas. Educational change does not always wait upon new administrative arrangements. So it is now time to look at this stage of education as a whole and to see what secondary education really means. We have already seen how the new methods in schools rest upon a number of principles. It is no longer rigidly divided into self-contained subjects; it arises most naturally and profitably from the interests of the pupils themselves; and the pupils are given the initiative in their own education. But all this is true of education at all levels. What are the specific characteristics of secondary education?

As good a place to start as any is the official Hadow report from as long ago as 1927. This was called "The Education of the Adolescent", and it gives us a clue to what secondary education is about. Adolescence is a time of great physical, mental and emotional changes: it is a time of becoming adult. At this stage children come to have adult interests and to grow into their adult capacities. The changes have been described in Chapter Three and if you have read the subsequent chapters with them in mind, much of the point of what secondary schools do will already be clear. You will have seen for example how provision for sports and physical education, for art and crafts, meets the growing physical strength and skill; how the teaching of English or history can involve the understanding of human emotions and relationships; how the normal curiosity of childhood can become organized, with the appearance of a capacity for logical thought, and developed into an interest in science and scientific methods.

Growing up also involves coming to terms with reality. Young children often do not distinguish very well between phantasy and fact. Adolescence is a time of learning to reconcile one's wants and imagination to possibilities in the real world. The desire to do so is very strong and it leads young people to demand of their studies at school that they should be "realistic" or "relevant" to life. This can also mean specific preparation for jobs and careers.

Teachers have found that they can build upon these interests of the children to the great benefit of their education and development. We have seen that the curriculum is not limited by the interests of the pupils (that would be an almost anti-educational procedure) but it does arise out of them. It is for this reason that there is very much less concern to "cover" a syllabus. (Human knowledge is expanding so fast that this is a forlorn attempt anyway.) It also implies the end to subject boundaries that we have already noticed.

Becoming an adult involves accepting responsibility, and young people face it with mixed feelings, being at the same time eager and uncertain. The schools increasingly try to give them experience in it. They not only do so in small things, but decisions about learning. Within a particular class there will be much less instruction and demonstration from the teacher and much more experiment, research and writing up by the pupils. And over the whole curriculum, pupils are increasingly encouraged to choose what its components should be.

How does this work out in practice? In the first place, the schools try to think of the secondary course as a whole. At present, that course is for half the children only four years long, and many of them leave before the end of the fourth year. This means in effect that teachers try to create a four year course which will be coherent and up to a point self-contained. One must not overdo this idea of a continuous course. At every age, the material has to be suitable for the pupils and relevant to their ends and interests. A year is a long time to a teenager, and it is no use offering material whose point will become clear only a year or two later. Many old syllabuses seem to be constructed on the principle that a child's memory is prodigious. They started, in history for instance, with the old stone age, when the children were eleven, and proceeded through the Assyrians, the Romans, mediaeval man and Elizabethan England to the heyday of empire in the nineteenth century. This kind of course may look coherent on paper, but its coherence may not be too obvious to the pupils. What today's teachers try to do is to see both that the material is suitable for the pupils attempting it and that each successive stage is part of an overall scheme to arouse interest, deepen understanding and widen knowledge.

A clue about the way teachers think may be gained from their reaction to the idea of raising the school leaving age. Many parents talk of this as providing an extra year. To teachers this is to miss the point. They see the problem, not as adding an extra year to the existing course, but of rethinking and recasting the whole work of the secondary schools in a new five-year course. The opportunities are enormous. We remember from Chapter Three the new possibilities which are opened when young people continue their full time education through adolescence. Briefly it means that they can be offered an education appropriate to young adults, not one which is appropriate only to children. A course coherently planned over the years of adolescence, matching at each step the developing potential of the pupils, can begin to offer, perhaps for the first time in Britain, preparation for life which aspires to adequacy.

One of the difficulties which the new secondary schools face is that they accommodate children of all kinds and levels of ability. Indeed, part of the purpose of re-organizing secondary education is to avoid separating pupils into different kinds of schools. We have seen that such evidence as there is suggests that this can be beneficial for less able pupils without hindering the development of the most able. The gathering of children together in one school may solve one problem, but it obviously creates others of its own. Can one think of offering the same course both to the more and less able? Does not offering pupils material suitable to their own abilities and stage of development require that pupils get quite different treatment? A number of anxieties about comprehensive schools centre round these questions.

The difficulties are the easiest to see if you look at each end of the ability range. There are children who show extremely high ability. Some of them excell in a particular subject or field. Musical or mathematical prodigies are not all that rare. A school which hopes to do justice to the needs of all pupils has to take these children into account. (Bertrand Russell, for example, believed that teaching such children alongside others is an extreme form of cruelty to them.).

On the other hand, there are children in schools whose abilities, measured in any of the normal ways, are extremely limited. There may be many reasons for this, including a depressed neighbourhood and lack of home support. We saw in Chapter Three how a child's capacities depended upon the interaction of his heredity and his environment. There is a continuing debate about the best way of helping the severely poor. There are, for example, special schools for the educationally sub-normal, just as there are for children with specific handicaps, like blindness or deafness. But probably the trend of opinion is in favour of accepting these children into the normal schools. There, they too need treatment which is appropriate to them. It may be no good flinging them in with the rest and letting them sink or swim. And parents need not forget that normal children, those whose abilities are neither on one extreme nor the other, also need an education which is appropriate to them. It is easier to offer this, not less important to do so.

Chapter Four has shown how schools try to meet some of these problems. Most of them "stream" children by ability. The children in any one year are divided into groups according to some sort of judgment about their capacities. Most teachers favour this. They say that arranging for the teaching groups to contain similar children enables their particular needs to be met. Probably most cannot imagine how to do justice to individuals in classes containing a very wide range of ability. It seems to them inevitable that the most able must be held back and the least able be neglected. Against this there is the growing feeling among a minority of teachers that streaming perpetuates within a school disadvantages of selection between schools. These teachers feel that the new methods and approaches enable a class of a wide range of ability to function happily and well, and it is clear that the further you get from lecturing a group as a whole, the nearer you come to encouraging each child to be responsible for his own work, the more likely it is that you can do justice to all the children in an unstreamed class.

What a number of schools do is to stream only the extremes of the ability range. In other words, most children in a school are not streamed and each class has a broad range of ability. But the very ablest pupils and the least able are each grouped in a stream of their own.

We have seen, too, in Chapter Four, how schools may not only divide children into streams, but also divide them into "sets". A set means grouping children not according to their overall abilities, but according to their ability in particular subjects. A boy may be in the ablest set for French and the least able for mathematics. This avoids the kind of overall judgment about children which teachers are increasingly reluctant to make, and many schools are combining a system of setting with mixed ability classes. Normally this means that the executant subjects— mentioned in Chapter Nine—are the ones in which streaming can be most easily abolished. At any rate it is thought that children of all kinds of ability can collaborate best in physical education, the arts, handicraft and home economics, where it might be difficult for them to do so in mathematics. It is probably safe to guess that the experience of teachers in the executant subjects will show more and more teachers of academic subjects how to deal wel! with mixed ability groups. The move towards ending rigid divisions by ability is not ended yet.

One of the pressures behind it is the feeling that a secondary education must contain a minimum content for all children. There are no longer regulations which lay down what a secondary education should consist of, but there is a feeling that if it is to be secondary in more than name it should include mathematics, science and a foreign language, as well as English, history, physical education, arts, handicraft and the rest. We have seen what the pressures are to make, say, a foreign language available to all pupils regardless of ability. There is clearly a limit to the extent to which all pupils can or ought to follow the same course. What the schools try to do is to create a "common core" of subjects which all pupils take. Gradually, and partly in the later years, they can choose additional subjects or concentrate on a group of subjects within the common core. The object is to give children a good all-round general education, but to encourage them to specialize and study in greater depth their chosen specialisms. Most children may take a basic course of English and social studies, mathematics and science, art and physical education, but as they get older, some may find that between the third and half of their time is taken up by their specialist interest. A child concentrating on English and social studies may find himself doing less mathematics—and so on. Here again the school's object will be to create for each pupil or group of pupils a course which is coherent within itself. The fashionable word today is "integrated". What it means is that a school will try to offer not just a collection of subjects but a course in which each subject is a relevant and consistent part. For example, in a course based on English, modern languages and social studies, the science might be centred round human biology and the mathematics biased towards logic.

Of course, there is a sense in which children who are specializing need to be kept in touch with that part of human knowledge and endeavour which is most different from their speciality. The argument here is that a child who is concentrating on the sciences, say, particularly needs a humanizing contact with the arts. Someone

specializing in the social sciences particularly needs to understand technology. How this is done is a matter of judgment.
What teachers have found is that trying to introduce
children to the opposite of their central interest produces
not so much a breadth of education as plain boredom. More
and more of them are coming to see that here as in so much
else the need is to start (though not also to end) with the
interests of the children themselves.

What these different courses and specialisms imply for
children is choice. In the primary schools children follow a
common curriculum without question. They tackle what
the teacher gives them. Of course, within the overall syllabus,
the children do have initiative. They work at their own
pace and on what most interests them. But in the secondary
school this initiative is taken further and made more formal.
At various stages children will be required to choose what
course they take. This might happen quite early. In the
second year, for example, a child may be asked to choose
between French and German. In the third year he may be
offered the choice between concentrating on the biological
and the technological sciences. By the fourth year the choice
may be much more drastic. He may be asked to settle for a
particular bias for his whole work. He will choose, in other
words, the centre of his studies round which his whole
course will be based. The divisions here will be very broad,
based upon science or "arts" (English, languages, etc.) but
the combinations of particular subjects offered may be
legion.

It would be right to say that there is a good deal of
disquiet in the country about these fundamental choices.
Many people say that they have to be made too early. The
reason why they are made at the beginning of the fourth
year is that the schools may offer a two-year course leading
to external examinations like the General Certificate of
Education. (see page 111 below). But the age of fourteen
is in most ways too early for people to take a decision which
may affect not only their education for the next two, four
or even eight years (if they go to higher education) but their
whole careers and lives. Similarly, many people have

complained that the nation's supply of skilled manpower rather idiotically depends upon the choice made by fourteen year olds. British education, like that of most of Western Europe, gives a very high priority to early academic attainment. It therefore demands specialization and this is intensified by the competition for places in universities and colleges. The schools, while recognizing the difficulties, do not quite see how to meet them. The best of them try to see that no decision is entirely irrevocable, by keeping children in touch with those subjects in which they are not specializing. Few of them would claim any large degree of success in this.

The burden which a degree of choice places upon the schools is that of guidance and counselling. We shall have more to say about vocational guidance in Chapter Fourteen. For the moment, it is enough to say that schools are becoming aware of a large gap in their provision where counselling ought to be. When children are offered a choice, they do not take it unaided or uninfluenced. Usually the school offers a rough and ready guide to them, and may even itself limit the choice available. For example, a child deciding whether or not to take a second foreign language may be quite bluntly told by his teacher that there is no sense in it because he is no good at the first. He is perhaps more likely to be gently advised that his poor performance in the first should suggest to him that he should not embark upon a second. This may seem obvious, in a commonsense sort of way, but it need not always be right. A child who is no good at German for example may get quite a long way with Italian. In other fields, this sort of criterion can be even less relevant. For example, pupils are often persuaded to give up science because their mathematics are weak. The reason for this is that most sciences demand a good grounding in mathematics. Often what is wanted, however, is remedial work on the mathematics, rather than closing off science to may pupils at an early age.

Most teachers would claim that although there are few formal counselling services in schools, the organisation of schools acts as an informal substitute for them. A child may have three or more teachers who are specifically responsible for keeping an eye on him. He may have a class teacher, a house teacher and specialist teachers for particular subjects. All of them can be relied upon to make a judgment about his progress both in detail and overall. Those who argue against a formal counselling service point to these inter-locking informal relationships. It remains true however that none of these teachers has a specific responsibility for advising, and perhaps more important is not particularly well equipped to do so. English schools still rely heavily upon tests of achievement in particular subjects, and we have seen that this can be unsatisfactory. In particular they are no guide at all to possible ability in fields which the pupil has not yet studied. English schools are still far behind their counterparts in America in the use of psycho-logical and other aptitude tests in the often tricky business of advising pupils on particular courses of study. The measures and methods used are still pretty crude. Parents and pupils alike should bear this in mind when the schools become autocratic in their advice. There are stirrings of a movement for change, but as these are growing from feelings of inadequacy about careers' advice, they will be dealt with more fully in the next chapter.

Examinations

Almost all schools test or examine. They do so for a number of reasons. Teachers themselves feel that they need some sort of check on how much children are actually learning. Of course, this can be noticed informally, in the course of supervising work in progress. In fact the more active children are in their own education, the easier it is for teachers to see their strengths and weaknesses. Schools also feel the need to measure the achievement of pupils against each other. This may be done for setting or streaming, and here they need a more formal measure. It is not enough to have a general idea about a pupil's progress when you are deciding between that pupil and another very similar. The need here is to get the pupils to display their attainments in a comparable fashion: hence the test or examination. Many teachers also feel that tests are an important educational incentive. Human beings, and their young, are naturally competitive. Set them a hurdle and most of them will jump it. It may be ideally desirable that children should learn because of the strength of their interest in the subject. But of course interest may flag, and the external pressure of preparing for a test may encourage learning that otherwise might be neglected. The public has an interest too. Parents need to know how their children are getting on at school. Many schools welcome them in on sufficient occasions for them to see the consequences of their children's normal work in their exercise books, projects and other performances. But parents need more than this. They need to know not only that their child is developing and is thus capable of more this year than he was last year, but also how his development compares with that of his contemporaries. They too need to know about his strengths and weaknesses. The formal test or examination is one obvious way of doing this. The community at large also needs to have some indication that the schools are doing their job. To a very large extent it takes the schools' word for it, but it is comforted if the schools can offer some recognizable and formal measure of what their pupils are achieving.

The argument against tests is that they are extremely crude devices. They measure very little, mostly memory and the speed of reaction that people call intelligence. They may also measure quite different things without distinguishing between them. For example, one child, with a retentive memory and a quick grasp of new material, may sail almost effortlessly through an examination for which another child may have prepared laboriously and with effort. Yet both children may secure the same mark in the examination. What, then, has been measured? It is becoming generally accepted that a very great deal more work needs to be done on the whole business of examining and testing in schools. A start has been made, by the Schools Council and others, but it is only a start. The disadvantage which our present crude examinations involve is that the test comes to dominate the curriculum. One wants an examination to make a judgment on what has been taught and learnt. The initiative should be with the teacher. What can too easily happen is that the examination in fact determines what is taught, and this can often mean that the syllabus becomes more and more removed from the needs of the pupils. The dilemma is a general one. It is in the interests of pupils that their education should be of a high standard, yet too rigid a concern with standards can destroy education.

The dilemmas about examinations are sharpened when the examinations themselves are set not by the schools but by outside bodies. The examination which a school sets and marks itself, called an "internal" examination, can clearly arise naturally from the needs of teaching and of the pupils. The examination set outside the school, an "external" examination, may obviously be remote and inflexible and may come to dominate the curriculum rather than serve it. On the other hand, the external examination gives pupils, their parents, teachers and the community at large a nationally valid standard by which their education can be measured. The attempt to resolve these dilemmas has dominated discussion about examinations for very many years, and is reflected in the actual structure of examinations. It also leads to periodic proposals from the Schools Council and other bodies for new patterns of examinations.

General Certificate of Education: The General Certificate of Education, the GCE as it is universally known, has hitherto been the most important external examination in secondary schools. The first examining boards were founded by the universities over 100 years ago, and the universities still run six of the eight GCE boards which now exist. Each board makes its own syllabus, sets its own question papers and publishes lists of results. This means that the types of papers set vary from one board to another and the schools thus have some choice in the kinds of syllabuses they adopt. It is also widely said that standards between the different boards vary considerably, but the boards themselves take trouble to see that their standards are comparable. Overall responsibility for the GCE lies with the Schools Council.

The GCE was established in its present form in 1951. It replaced the old General School Certificate and the Higher School Certificate examinations. The change was significant because it introduced the distinctive feature of the GCE. The old school certificate demanded passes in specific groups of subjects: if a pupil did not have the right number and combination of these, he did not get a certificate. The GCE is what is called a "subject" examination: that is, a pupil gets a certificate recording whatever passes he may have attained regardless of whether he has nine of these or only one. The change was made to give schools more flexibility, to recognize attainment in subjects other than the obligatory ones of the school certificate, and to offer incentives to a wider range of candidates. The standard of the examination was also raised. The old school certificate had three grades of award: pass, credit and distinction. The passmark in the GCE is comparable with the credit of the old school certificate.

Many people ask what virtue there is in a certificate with only one subject on it. To this there are two answers. The first is that it is better for a child to achieve in one thing than in nothing. The second is that the one subject might represent a qualification to an employer or for admission to a further course in a technical college or elsewhere. Behind the objection to the subject examination lies the feeling that the old demand for a specific number of subjects in specific combinations guaranteed a general education. For example, the mathematician on the way to a brilliant distinction knew that he had to get at least a pass in English and perhaps a foreign language if he were to get a certificate. The obverse of this argument is that this means withholding recognition of one achievement just because somebody has not gained another. The argument continues, but meanwhile vastly more children are in fact achieving the old certificate standards.

The GCE examination is held at two levels, ordinary—

O level—and advanced—A level. Pupils normally take O level at the end of their fifth year in a secondary school, that is at about the age of 16. They take A level after two years in a sixth form, that is about the age of 18. But candidates may enter for different subjects at different dates and may enter for the same more than once. They may build up a number of subjects on their certificate over a number of years. In some schools pupils may ignore O level altogether in those subjects which they will take at A level.

Passes in individual subjects at A level are credited A to E in descending order of merit and candidates who fail at A level may be awarded an O level pass if their performance warrants it. The A level candidates in a particular subject may attempt "special" papers in this subject. Passes are not awarded in these papers, but candidates can earn supplementary grading of "distinction" or "merit". The A level grades and supplementary gradings are taken into account by universities and colleges offering places and by local authorities in awarding scholarships.

Most boards hold O and A level examinations in the summer and a second O level in the autumn. Two boards have a second A level—in January. Between 40 and 50 subjects or groups of subjects are normally taken at O level and 40 at A level. The most popular single subject at O level is English, followed by mathematics. The least popular is ancient history. The most popular single subject in A level is also English, closely followed by physics. On the other hand at A level there are several different kinds of mathematics papers, and the total number of candidates for maths of all kinds is rather more than for English. The pass rate in different subjects can vary quite considerably, but on the whole something over half of the candidates at O level and two-thirds of those at A level gain passes.

The importance of the GCE lies in the fact that success in it at some level is accepted as a minimum qualification for entry to universities, colleges, and professional courses. In general the universities' minimum entry requirements are five or six O levels and two A levels. Satisfying these minimum requirements does not however guarantee a place at a university. Competition for places means that individual universities in practice have plenty of people with more than the nimimum requirements to choose from. And particular faculties or departments of universities may insist on a certain standard in their own or other subjects.

Certificate of Secondary Education: Since the summer of 1965 GCE has been joined by a new examination, the Certificate of Secondary Education, or CSE. This new examination arose directly from the argument about the place of examinations in education. There were already objections that the GCE inhibited the better work done in schools by making it too formal, academic, inflexible and stereotyped. For every teacher who argued that there should be some examination to measure achievement of those who could not manage the GCE, there were other teachers who resisted the extension of examinations to growing numbers of pupils.

The CSE was constructed so as to meet many of the objections to examinations. Unlike the GCE, its governing councils, examinations committees and subject planners of its 14 regional examining bodies all have a majority of teachers from schools affected by the examination. What is more, the examination has three "modes", offering a choice of initiative to teachers. In the first mode schools submit their candidates for the regional examining boards' examinations. In the second, schools or groups of schools put up their own examination schemes for approval by the examining boards. In the third, the examinations are set and marked internally by the individual schools or groups of schools, and are moderated only by the boards. It is this third mode which gives teachers most freedom. They can meet the needs of their pupils directly: indeed, this mode amounts to an internal examination. On the other hand, pupils, teachers, parents and employers have the same assurances that an external examination can give. Moderation by the boards assures the validity of the personal work and relationships as the schools. It would be pleasing to report that teachers have rushed to accept the opportunities offered by mode three. Alas, fewer than one in ten of the candidates are as yet entered for examinations in this mode. It seems that it will take time for teachers to gain sufficient confidence to run directly their own examinations.

Like the GCE the CSE is a subject examination. You can get a certificate with only one subject on it and there is no limit to the subjects you can offer. But the CSE is also branching out into more practical subjects like building and engineering science, civics and typewriting. There is no pass or fail line in the CSE. Results are given for each subject in five grades—one to five—or are ungraded. Grade one is meant to indicate a standard comparable to a pass at GCE O level. Grade four is meant to suggest a standard to be expected of a 16-year old of average ability, who has conscientiously pursued an appropriate course in the subject; and grades two and three, as might be expected, fall between these two. Grade five is meant to show that the candidate performed well enough to suggest that it was right for him to enter for the examination, but not high enough to get a grade four. Candidates who do not qualify for grade five are ungraded, and the implication is that they were really not up to standard. You can see that these gradings are an attempt to be somewhat more subtle than the results of GCE. In particular, the concept that a pupil is of a standard which would suggest he should enter for the examination is a useful one.

A pupil gets his certificate of secondary education if he can put on it more than one grade between one and four. If he gets nothing but grade five, in however many subjects, he does not get a certificate. On the other hand, if he gets a certificate, any grade fives he gets are entered on it. All candidates are told about their results, including ungradings, but these notices are not the same as a certificate.

We have seen that the standard of the CSE overlaps with that for GCE: CSE grade one and O level are comparable. It is generally held resonable that one in five of all the pupils in an age group can attempt GCE and that the next two in five can go for CSE. This means that there are external examinations in secondary schools for pupils from the academically most able to those of just below average ability. General satisfaction with this state of affairs is mitigated by the realisation that nearly a half of the pupils in schools may never aspire to a nationally recognized qualification.

One of the most important aspects of the new CSE is that it offers a way into education after school which is different from the old GCE. The latter is designed to be suitable for academic pupils. The CSE is designed to be more relevant to the needs of all pupils. In the past a non-academic pupil might well be inhibited from pursuing his studies by the fact that the only examination available to him was an academic one. Today he can take the CSE and, if he does well in it, can achieve a grading comparable in standard to GCE O level. This can be his springboard to the sixth form and to further and higher education. It is not surprising perhaps that teachers and others are already discussing the extension of the CSE principle to a new examination comparable in standard with GCE A level.

The Sixth Form

All the pupils staying on at school after 16 are said to be in the "sixth-form", divided into the first and the second year sixth. Traditionally they have followed a two year course leading to GCE A level, which has been dominated by the demands of university entrance, even though perhaps most pupils were not going on to university. In the schools themselves there has always been a sharp distinction made between the sixth form and what was characteristically called the "main school". This distinction arose from the nature of the sixth. In the first place, it was composed entirely of pupils who were at school voluntarily, and this will still be the case even after the school leaving age is raised to sixteen. Almost all other children at school are there because they have to be: sixth formers are there because they want to be. This profoundly affects their attitudes and those of their teachers to the work which they are doing.

Traditionally, too, the sixth form attitude to work has been academic. This has been held to mean a concentrated study "in depth" of a relatively restricted range of subjects. This concentration is held to be of educational value. In contrast with the extremely broad and general courses of his American contemporary, the English sixth former's curriculum may be concentrated on mathematics and a science or two or three modern languages. It is admitted that as an education this is very narrow, but those who defend it argue that it makes possible a thoroughness and an attention to detail which characterizes the academic approach. The word for this is "depth".

More practically, the sixth form course concentrates on a narrow range of subjects in order to meet the demands of university entrants. Faced with applications from growing numbers of potential students, the universities have responded by raising their entry requirements. This has meant that the standards required can be reached only by single-mindedness and concentration. To broaden the curriculum in present circumstances would be to jeopardize pupils' chances of higher education.

A third characteristic of the sixth form is the extent to which pupils themselves are responsible for their own work. In the past this was often more evident than it is today. The ideal was to fill half or less of a pupil's time table with formal lessons and to leave the other half free for private study. Under the pressure of examinations the time table has become fuller—and the narrowness which this creates has been thought to be mitigated by timetabling still more, culturally important, subjects. Even so, it is still true that a sixth former has a good deal more control over the amount and kind of work that he does than has a pupil in the main school or even than some university students. His relationship with his teachers becomes quite different. In the most successful schools it can approach that of scholar and disciple. A sixth former may be inspired by even a chance phrase to pursue some line of investigation—and he will be encouraged to do so. It is in one sense a part of the process of growing up. At the age of 17 or 18 a pupil cannot be treated like a child, cannot indeed be treated like a pupil. Especially in these days he demands intellectual and social equality. This may be made even more obvious by his sharing in the organization and running of the school, as head of his house or as a school prefect, as chairman of a school group or society or captain of a school team. To the more junior pupils of the school he may seem quite as much part of the establishment as the staff.

Perhaps the most obvious fact about the sixth form is that most children do not enter it. Only one in four does so and perhaps a half or more of these do a full two-year course. Some of the others do get some form of further education, as we shall see, but the traditional English sixth form accommodates most of those who are going to university, college and professional occupations. For good or ill, these pupils will have had an educational experience unknown to the rest.

The arguments against the sixth form have become increasingly insistent in recent years. Its needs are said to dominate the curriculum of the fourth and fifth forms, making these unnecessarily narrow and specialist, just as the sixth forms themselves are dominated by the demands of the universities. In particular the sixth forms are said to give way too easily to the overloading of the curriculum. The science subjects, in particular, are making increasingly heavy demands, but the trend is a general one. Perhaps most important, the traditional sixth form is unattractive to large numbers of pupils. The two-year course to A level, for example, is not universally suitable. Some pupils could do with a shorter, perhaps vocationally biased, course, but in the traditional school these needs are either not accommodated or are accepted grudgingly and treated as a second best.

As schools become comprehensive the nature of the sixth form is bound to change. The demands of the universities are continuingly insistent, and all schools will have to cope with them as best they can, but going comprehensive means enlarging the scope of the sixth form and extending the opportunities for continued education to very much larger groups of pupils. Oddly enough, this broadening of the range of work offered has taken place more often in girls' schools than in boys'. This is because there have been several well recognized professions for girls which recruit at 18 without insisting (as yet) on A level passes or the equivalent. This has meant that shorthand and typing, pre-nursing courses and the like have been introduced alongside a general education for girls pursuing their education after 16. It is likely that this kind of course will be increasingly introduced for boys as more and more occupations come to recruit at 18 rather than 16.

Indeed as the new secondary schools become more common, the sixth form will radically change. The old idea that only a tiny minority of children were capable of an academic course has quite rightly been exploded, but this does not mean that such a course is the only or indeed the right one for most children. No doubt growing numbers will take A level as a route to university and college, but many more are likely to take different courses perhaps with a pre-professional or vocational bias. This development is not yet particularly extensive, but it will become more common in the next few years. A number of people have wondered, in view of the different needs of the new sixth formers, whether it might not be better for young people of 17 and 18 to be educated in technical colleges and other colleges of further education rather than in schools. Of the arguments for this, the one relating to young people suggests that a school must inevitably have an attitude and indeed rules which relate to younger children, and that young people might prefer the more adult atmosphere of the colleges. Another argument is that at a time of shortage it is not economically sensible to have small classes in both schools and technical colleges, where large numbers of youngsters already take GCE courses. In this view it would be better for the colleges and schools to share the work at this level. At present there are virtually no formal arrangements of this kind, but again it is a development which is likely to grow.

One version of it is the "sixth form college." This is one of the ways of "going comprehensive" approved by the Department of Education and Science in its Circular 10/65. All the children of an area, in a scheme of this sort, go to comprehensive schools until they are 16 (which will soon be the school leaving age) and those who stay on do so in a separate institution, a sixth form or junior college. There are a number of areas where such colleges already exist, and the idea of them will almost certainly spread. It is claimed for them that if they offer an atmosphere much more suited to the young people themselves than that of a traditional school, and that the absence of the sixth form in the lower schools gives more scope for responsibility to those pupils who may be leaving at the earliest possible age.

On the other hand, some teachers fear that the attractiveness of teaching in a sixth form college may lure away specialists from the lower schools so that the quality of education there may suffer. And there are many people who are reluctant to see a change of school coinciding with the school leaving age. This, they feel, will stop some pupils from staying on, when they might have been persuaded to do so had it meant staying at the same school with which they had become familiar. Partly for this reason, and partly because it fits in better with the available buildings, one or two authorities have thought in terms of upper schools taking pupils from 14 or 15 to 18. This gets over the school leaving age problem, but may create others for the preparation for O level and CSE. On the other hand it does seem to offer added possibilities for the range and variety of courses for the middle and older pupils.

In the schools themselves a very great deal of thought has been given to the creation of a more adult atmosphere for sixth formers. In some schools this has gone a very long way, giving them, if not a separate college, at least a block or wing of the building to themselves. In it they may have a common room, library, study rooms and so on. Some of the more Victorian rules about uniform are relaxed, and some schools are even accepting the growing distaste among sixth formers for the exercise of petty authority over younger children.

All this means that the sixth form can increasingly be said to have a "collegiate" atmosphere, though it is fair to add that some of the sixth formers themselves may not entirely relish their isolation from the rest of the school. On the other hand, the isolation of academic pupils from the rest of their contemporaries may slowly be coming to an end. The new sixth form will contain youngsters of a wide range and variety of abilities pursuing various kinds of courses. This social mixing is held by some advocates of comprehensive schools to be one of their most important aspects.

Something of the flavour of the new sixth forms may be gained from the following extracts from a leaflet compiled for parents by Gordano School, Somerset. It is a successor to the two booklets quoted in Chapter Four. After outlining the academic and other courses available, the leaflet turns to more general matters.

Gordano School — The Upper School

The responsibilities of the sixth formers.

By the time pupils enter the Sixth they should realise that the more they put into the school the more they themselves will gain from it. This is true both of their academic studies and their cultural and social life in school.

A Sixth Former will find that he has one or two private study periods every day when he is not supervised by a member of staff. The use he makes of this time will greatly affect his performance in the external examinations. If he uses this time well he will not only pass the examinations but will also learn the secret of studying on his own. This will be of enormous benefit to him at University or when he is studying for a professional qualification. These free periods are not just in place of homework but in addition to it and no Sixth Former can do himself justice in an A level course unless he spends an average of one hour a night on each of his subjects.

The staff regularly organise visits to the theatre and

concerts and wise Sixth formers make the most of these visits. They should not however always rely entirely on the staff to select the best programmes and order the tickets but should acquire the habit of regular visits to the theatre or concerts on their own or with a few friends. I would urge parents to encourage such activities, which for a maturing citizen are a wise use of time and money in the broadening of their cultural experiences.

There are copies of many of the more serious newspaper and periodicals available in school, but this is the age at which young people should make the most of opportunities to buy magazines at cheap rates, start to distinguish between the responsible and sensational Sunday papers and begin to buy the books that will be the basis of their own library. All Sixth Formers will certainly have tickets for the public library where they can obtain almost any book they require either straight from the shelves or by ordering it from the County Library in Taunton.

The Social life of the Sixth Formers will centre around their own building, but many of them already help to organise useful activities for the younger pupils and by so doing gain enormous benefit themselves. At present there are the History Society, Mathematical Models Club, Christian Union, which are organised by the Sixth, but the number of these clubs is continually increasing.

Finally, the sixth formers have a responsibility to the community around the school in the valley—and beyond. Much very useful work in helping the old and infirm has already been done by the younger pupils of the school through "Helping Hands". The members of the Upper School should be prepared to help with this work, but as young adults should plan to take up the more ambitious tasks of which they are capable, and so take a lead in the community in which they live.

The new sixth form block.

For the last three years members of the sixth have worked hard and had few amenities or privileges. During the last year they have seen the Middle School move into their new house blocks and enjoy much better facilities than they have had. By September however the new block which has been specially designed to meet their needs should be ready. Here the students will have their own social area with their own kitchen and machine for hot drinks. There will be a social committee responsible for organising activities both inside and outside the normal school hours. The building also has small classrooms for advanced work, discussion rooms and study bays where students can work in comfort without formal supervision. It is hoped that in these very congenial surroundings the sixth formers may enjoy some of the freedom given to students in higher education, and thus find the transition from school to university, College of Education or industry harmonious and exciting.

The financial cost to parents.

There is no doubt that it costs every family a considerable amount of money to keep a son or daughter at school for the extra one or two years. Some parents at the moment are suffering very great financial hardship in order that one of their children may enjoy the benefits of the Sixth Form Course.

There are maintenance grants available on a graduated scale for parents whose income is less than £690. Full details of these grants can be obtained from the school or from the Chief Education Officer in Taunton.

These grants are not as much as the young person would earn, nor do they allow him to enjoy all the latest luxuries but they do enable those who would otherwise be unable to do so, to remain at school.

What pupils and parents want.

In all these chapters on the content of education we have been concerned with what the schools are offering. Time and again we have said that this arises out of the interests

E

of the pupils themselves. But what is it that the pupils want?
Fortunately there are some answers to this question which
come out of an inquiry carried out for the Schools Council
(see Chapter Thirteen) by the Government Social Survey.
The purpose of the inquiry was to help the schools to meet
the raising of the school leaving age. It set out to discover
the interests and motives of pupils between the ages of 13
and 16 and their views on what the schools were doing to
prepare them for adult life. It also sought to reveal both the
knowledge of teachers about what was relevant to their
pupils, and parents' views of their own and the schools'
roles in education.

The report (*Young School Leavers*—HMSO, price 15s.)
has very many more interesting facts in it than can be
summarized in this book, but there are some which are
central to this chapter. Take, for example, the question of
what a school is for. A representative number of 15 year old
school leavers and their parents were asked which of a
number of objectives of schools they considered very
important. Very broadly speaking most 15 year olds thought
objectives concerned with careers to be very important.
Slightly fewer of them thought that other practical aspects
of everyday life like money management and running a
home were very important. Slightly fewer again rated
highly the objective of self development (becoming independent, making the most of one's self and so on). Only
about one in three of the children rated highly the objective
of broadening the mind and developing interests and awareness.

To take some more typical examples, when asked which
school objectives were very important, 86 per cent of the
boys and 88 per cent of the girls plumped for "teaching
things which will help you to get as good a job or career as
possible" and 81 per cent chose "teach you things which
will be of direct use to you in your job". Other career
objectives were chosen as most important by 60 per cent
or more of both boys and girls. Similarly, 78 per cent of
boys and 83 per cent of girls picked as very important
"teach you how to manage your money when you are

earning and about things like rates and Income Tax". 78 per cent of girls picked "teach you things that will be useful in running a home, for example, about bringing up children, home repairs, decorating". Of both boys and girls 72 per cent chose "teach you to put things in writing easily". In all, over one half of the 15 year old school leavers chose help in these practical aspects of everyday life as very important objectives of schools. (There was one slightly odd exception: only 30 per cent of boys and 45 per cent of girls thought it important for the schools to give sex education. Presumably they thought they knew about it already).

Among the self development objectives 66 per cent of boys chose "help you to become independent and able to stand on your own feet" and "teach you about what is right and wrong". More of the girls chose these objectives: 76 per cent for right and wrong and 75 per cent for independence. Overall one half or more of both boys and girls thought self development an important objective of schools. The contrast with the arousal of interests and awareness is stark. None of these were rated as very important by as many as half the children. Some 45 per cent of girls and 38 per cent of boys picked "teach you plenty of subjects so that you can be interested in a lot of things": 32 per cent of boys and 23 per cent of girls chose "give you interests and hobbies that you can do in your spare time". Only 4 per cent of boys and 8 per cent of girls chose "study poetry in school and read and learn poems".

There is some evidence in the inquiry that these views about the important things a school does change as the pupils themselves grow older and have more experience of the world. In particular, 19 to 20 year olds were less likely to feel direct use in jobs was very important and would have rated higher the development of their own capabilities and interests.

The opinions of parents on the whole backed up those of the pupils—except that 91 per cent of parents of both boys and girls put "teach you to be able to put things in writing easily" as very important, and 90 per cent of girls' parents chose "teach you to speak well and easily". Similarly as many as 68 per cent of boys' parents and 69 per cent of girls' parents chose "run clubs that you can go to out of school hours"—one of the interets and awareness group so neglected by their children. On the whole more parents thought that all school objectives were important than did their children!

The views of teachers, on the other hand, were the direct reverse of both parents and pupils. Most of them claimed aspects of self development as very important and many of them chose from the interests and awareness group. Only a half or fewer thought that school objectives related to careers were very important. One exception to this general rule was "that the second largest number of teachers thought speaking well was an important objective. For the rest both heads and other teachers stressed the schools' contribution to personality and character, independence, confident behaviour and moral training. Some parents may be astonished to discover that few heads or teachers put examination achievement high on their list of important objectives. Only 19 per cent thought exams very important.

What all these figures suggest is that schools and pupils are far from being at one in their estimate of what school is for. Both the 15 year olds and their parents thought that school ought to provide knowledge and skills to enable young people to get the best jobs and careers. Teachers on the whole did not accept the achievement of vocational success as a major objective of education. What most of them thought important was the development of character and personality, the inculcation of ethical values and the maturing of personal relationships. The school leavers and their parents generally supported this except that neither saw personality and character development as a main responsibility of the schools. The 15 year olds also normally approved of instruction in the practical aspects of living, like managing money, being able to spell well and to put things into writing. Many fewer of them attached importance to the development of their interests and increasing their awareness of what was happening in the world.

These views are also reflected in what the pupils thought of their school subjects. The inquiry has an interesting table classifying school subjects under "useful" and "useless", and dividing each of these into "interesting" and "boring". More than half the boys found metalwork, woodwork and English both useful and interesting. Only slightly fewer of them made the same judgment on mathematics, science, physical education and commerce, technical drawing and geography. Between 20 and 40 per cent thought the same of current affairs, art and handicraft, foreign languages and history. Between 10 and 20 per cent thought maths, foreign languages and English useful but boring. Just over one in ten thought art and handicraft useless but interesting. Between 10 and 20 per cent thought history, art and handicraft and current affairs useless and boring and the same judgment was given by 30 and 26 per cent respectively for religious instruction and foreign languages. The accolade for uselessness and boredom went to music, judged to be so by half the boys.

The judgments of the girls were not significantly different overall. More than half found English and practical subjects like housecraft, commerce and needlework both useful and interesting. A similar number to the boys found maths and foreign languages useful but boring, and art and handicraft useless but interesting. With them too the accolade for uselessness and boredom went to music, though only a third of them judged it to be so. The major oddity with the girls was the finding that one in five of them regarded religious instruction as useful and interesting. Perhaps the most cheerful sign in all this for the schools is that very many more of the children were prepared to say that their school work was interesting than claimed it to be boring. Many more regarded their school work as useful than useless.

Parents tended to agree with their sons and daughters. More than two thirds of the parents of boys thought that English, mathematics, technical subjects and physical education were important at school and over three quarters of the girls' parents plumped for domestic subjects, English

and mathematics. One of the most constructive replies
from the children was to questions about the subjects they
wished they were better at. Substantial proportions of them
wished they were better at mathematics and English. A
number of them offered suggestions for helping this
improvement, including more lessons in the subjects they
considered inportant, more practical work and so on. But
an appreciable number of them simply blamed their own
lack of ability and assumed that nothing could be done to
help them—a quiet but damning indictment of their
education.

Asked what additional subjects they would choose if they
became available, the largest proportion of boys (say one in
six or seven) went for engineering subjects and foreign
languages. Interestingly enough, nearly a quarter of the
older 19 to 20 year olds said they would like to have learnt
foreign languages. Among the girls foreign languages were
mentioned as an additional subject by about a quarter,
about the same number as for commercial subjects.

These inquiries were made, of course, before the reorganization of secondary schools on comprehensive lines
got under way, but the attitude of parents, of pupils and
teachers cannot have changed very much. The results of the
inquiry show that the schools have quite a long way to go
before what they are trying to do is properly valued by their
pupils. But it is as good a place to end this section as any
to refer to what the inquiry discovered about the attitude
of parents to the changed approaches and methods in the
schools—changes which will spread more quickly as the
schools themselves become comprehensive. According to
the results of the inquiry, parents were very well aware that
schools had changed greatly since their own day. What they
most valued in the new schools were the wider and more
interesting curricula, better buildings and equipment,
more trouble taken with pupils, a better standard of work
and a happy atmosphere in schools. Some, of course, felt
that the changes were not altogether for the better and a
very few considered the schools less good than in their own
day. Both of these groups were critical of laxer discipline

and the lack of control of pupils' behaviour. Some also felt that too little attention was now paid to mastering the basic subjects, like reading writing and arithmetic. What all this suggests is that the movement towards the new secondary schooling does broadly command the support of parents.

Relations with parents.

The schools may be, generally, gratified by parental acceptance: few of them report parental hostility to what they are doing. But teachers in the secondary schools are coming to wonder whether they might not involve parents more in what the schools are doing. There is a great contrast here between the primary and secondary schools. The former have for some time sought to build upon the natural interest of parents in their children's early years of schooling to welcome them into the business of education. But the Schools Council inquiry found that only about one in three parents of children in the middle years (third, fourth and fifth) of secondary schools had a "real talk" with the head or other teachers. (A real talk was something more than passing the time of day). What is also interesting is that the earlier a child left school, the less likely was his parent to have had a talk with a teacher.

This lack of contact need not necessarily stem from a lack of parental concern for their children's welfare and progress: it may be rooted in definite attitudes to children's development and education. In the first place, some parents seem to feel that responsibility for education is the business of the school and that they should not intervene unless there is trouble. Second, parents often feel that they are interfering, or might be thought to be, if they went up to the school uninvited. Such parents often wish there were more opportunities in the way of school functions to which they might go. Third, many parents feel uncertain of themselves when they go in to schools and wonder whether they would be able to have a satisfactory conversation with teachers if they wanted to.

On the other hand the lack of contact is being increasingly felt and regretted by both parents and teachers. A half of the parents of school leavers were anxious to be told more about how their children were getting on and a third of them felt that teachers should consult them more. Teachers equally considered that they could learn a lot from parents about the children and their backgrounds which would help them in teaching.

One of the ways in which the schools try to encourage parents to take an interest is in the provision of school functions, like school entertainments, speech days, sports days and so on. None of these occasions are very suitable for a long formal talk. In the first place, there are the plays, races, music, prize-giving and whatever—which are the main object of the function. Very often teachers are very busy taking a hand in these and may be hard put to it to remember one childs name let alone discuss him rationally. The best thing about these social functions is, first, that you get to know the school a bit, see the sort of work it does in these fields and get to know one or two teachers personally. From the point of view of serious discussion these functions may prepare the ground, help you to feel at ease and so on. Of course, if you see a teacher and can have a quick word you will find he will respond very readily—but if you want a solid talk arrange another meeting.

The most obvious occasion for this is the open day or evening. On these occasions the whole school is, as it were, on show. In the classrooms the pupils' work is displayed. In the laboratories and workshops imposing experiments or constructions are being prepared. There may be gymnastic displays, musical or dramatic performances and so on. At the same time, the teachers are available for any parent who may want to talk about his child's work. Sometimes schools simply set aside evenings when teachers are available without holding a formal open evening. This kind of arrangement often attracts quite a lot of parents to the schools, partly because they are formally invited and thus feel wanted. Of course, there is a limit to the amount of time a teacher can spend with any one parent, and if there is a queue of people behind you it is hard to have a relaxed chat about a nagging worry. But it is certainly adequate for many parents, and if there is something more to be said, arrange another meeting. We shall also see later how schools may also organize careers evenings, concerned with the future as well as with school work.

These open days are certainly appreciated by parents: the most frequent suggestion parents make about schools is that there should be more of them. Parents would also like the schools to fix days and times on which they could see parents without their making an appointment. On the other hand, many parents certainly feel intimidated by the thought of such interviews. This is mostly due to lack of practice: after all head teachers are pretty used to meeting parents; parents are not so used to meeting head teachers. The remedy is for parents actually to meet the heads; the second time is always easier and more profitable. And it really is a help to have met him on some other occasion, informally, beforehand: it makes him seem more human.

Parents who think the school should do more to welcome them may be amused to know how the situation looks to the teachers. In the Schools Council inquiry, half the heads and two thirds of the teachers thought that parents were not interested in what the schools were trying to achieve. It may be, of course, that more contact would reveal to the teachers more parental interest. At all events most of them thought that positive steps should be taken to encourage parents to visit schools frequently, though they were not all agreed about the best methods of doing this. Those teachers who wanted to make a point of getting the less interested parents to come to the schools were clear that one could not do it simply by having open days. More personal contacts, from invitations to visits to pupils homes, were needed.

One way in which barriers between parents and teachers can be broken down is in a school parents' association or parent teacher association. These vary enormously. Some are purely social clubs. Others are fund-raisers, providing fully equipped stages or swimming pools for the school, through summer fairs, jumble sales, raffles and the like. Probably most meet occasionally but regularly, hearing talks, brains trusts and the like, or enjoying social evenings. The difference between a parents' association and a parent teacher association is often purely formal. In the latter the teachers are likely to be represented on the committee of the association and so on. But neither kind of association can meet without the goodwill (or at least acquiescence) of the head teacher and his staff. If it exists it can be very helpful in providing a neutral ground where teachers and parents can meet, so that if they have to discuss a child there is no uncertainty and unfamiliarity to add to the problem which has arisen. It is clear that this is vitiated if the staff oppose the whole idea. So if you want to start up an association get together with other parents and sound out the head and staff. If they agree, you are well away.

But remember that in all this you and the teachers are cooperating for the benefit of the children. If you do find yourself having an argument with a teacher, remember that it is more important that you should come to a satisfactory arrangement about the child than that you should win the argument. The new pattern of learning includes consultation and cooperation with parents, giving life to the Act of Parliament which places the duty to see that children are educated directly upon them. Parents too can help to make this a reality.

CHAPTER TWELVE

Outside the classroom

At school meetings for parents you may have heard a head
say, somewhat sentimentally, that it is what goes on outside
the classroom that is the most important part of education.
I have often noticed parents looking a bit puzzled at this
point, especially since no explanation of this cryptic remark
is normally forthcoming. You can see them wondering
what on earth the whole apparatus of school and teachers,
subjects and curricula, new approaches, methods and the
rest are for, if what the head says is true. What he means, of
course, is somewhat different. The main business of schools
must always be concentrated in the classroom. This is
where pupils and teachers spend most of their time, this is
where (backed by the whole apparatus of Schools Council,
inspectors, advisers and all) have put their most concentrated professional effort. This experience which one can
only imperfectly describe and understand by looking at
timetables and syllabuses, is the main thing that schools
have to offer. But it is not the only thing. In Britain there
has been a long tradition that schools are not just teaching
shops; they are communities. This means that very many
teachers do much more than the formal timetable requires.
They may stay in the school buildings for hours after the
final bell, or spend much of their "holidays" on visits or
projects. There is another tradition, almost as venerable,
that for at least part of the time and in some circumstances
pupils may take responsibility for their own education. The
school, in other words, is more than just a collection of
classes, however well "integrated", and education is more
than classwork, however free and creative.

Perhaps you can now see what the headmaster really

means: he means that it is the *extra* activities and aspects which make all the difference. This is the sense in which they are important. If what happens in the classroom is unsatisfactory, no amount of outside activity will get things right. But if the classwork is good, what goes on outside the class can add a richness of experience which the classroom alone cannot give. (If the headmaster, and the rest of us, were more familiar than we are with economics, we should all have readily understood the idea of the "margin" —the extra—and how vitally important it can be).

What are these extra, "extra-curricular", "after-school", outside activities? One of the most important is not an activity at all, but what people call the "tone" of the school. Parents often think of this when they see a traditional school, with children neatly decked out in blazers, their faces bright and shiny and their manners improbable—like an old film. This is certainly one way of creating "tone" but it is not the only way. A school can do it quite as well without such regard to outer cleanliness, though many teachers claim that the job is harder. What is important is the morale of pupils and teachers. This stems from a sense of confidence, and is most soundly based when the head teacher and staff share clearly understood objectives, know how to attain them and work hard to do so. The objectives themselves may be very different. One school may seek uniformity among its pupils, another individuality. One staff may be formal and remote, another informal and friendly. Of course, there is nothing so conducive to confidence as success—which is the respectable reason for all those honours boards, cups and trophies—but a head who has other priorities can create confidence too, if his staff and pupils understand and share his vision.

Many teachers believe that morale and confidence are hard to create in large schools. Both depend on personal relationships, they feel, and large schools can be remote and impersonal. There may be something in this, but size also has its advantages. The range of work and opportunity a large school can offer may also raise the spirits. The crucial factors are the quality of staff and the way the school is organized, rather than size.

At all events it is widely accepted in Britain that a central part of the job of a head teacher and staff is to create a feeling of community which is much more than the sum total of all the subjects of study in the school. Many of the ways in which this is done, like morning assembly or house systems, are described elsewhere in this book. A school may also typically offer innumerable activities quite apart from the normal school timetable.

Among the most familiar of these are sports. A school may have first, second, third and junior teams for games like football, hockey and cricket. These teams play in the evenings and at weekends against teams from other schools, and they practice in the lunch hours and after school. Inter-school rivalry may generate a good deal of excitement, and the teams may be followed by faithful bands of spectators. A great deal of sports activity of this sort continues long after the end of the formal timetable. For the school athletics meeting in the summer term, which may well be held on a Saturday, boys may have trained during the evenings for weeks. Sports not represented on the normal timetable may also flourish after school. Fencing, swimming, judo, squash may all have clubs formed by even small groups of devotees.

Other clubs continue after hours the subjects of the curriculum: art, crafts, music, drama and so on. Some schools achieve memorable performances of Shakespearean or modern plays, or of great musical works like Handel's Messiah. Others put on regular art exhibitions. Many pupils make chairs, pottery and the like for themselves and their families. There may be history, maths, science or modern language clubs. One of the most common clubs is a debating society at which the members consider motions like "This house has no confidence in the Government" or "The growth of crime demands the reintroduction of capital punishment" or "The morals of the old should not affect the behaviour of the young." There is almost no sport, game or pastime that is not found in some school's extra-curricular activities: chess, pets, model engineering, Christian fellowship, dress design, Duke of Edinburgh's award, climbing, boat building, stamp and coin collecting, archeology. . . .

Nor do the meetings of these clubs and societies take place only in the school buildings. The climbing club may spend its weekends on Snowdon, the art club will visit galleries and museums, the French club may go to Paris. And some of the activities in the school can be extremely ambitious. One school runs a bank. Another works a computer.

More and more schools are also offering some form of social service. One of the most popular is service to the aged. Youngsters visit old people who may be lonely; shop for them, read to them, even decorate their homes. Another common activity is raising money for charities at home and abroad. Very often activities like sponsored walks are arranged by the senior boys and girls of a school.

There are a number of points about these out of school activities which set them apart from what happens in the classroom. The first is that they are voluntary. The children are pursuing their own interests because they want to do so, not because they are part of a set curriculum. Of course, the curriculum itself is increasingly related to these interests. And many of the clubs and societies continue and develop school subjects. But the clubs enable a child to take his interest further than may be possible in class. They enable him to concentrate, to specialise, even to "research."

Second, the clubs are most often run by the pupils themselves. This gives them the experience not only of organization—and democratic organization at that: there can be no compulsion in them—but of the intellectual structure of their interest. The children define what the club should do, and how it should go about it. Many parents are surprised at the organizing ability of which even the youngest secondary school pupils are capable. But this experience in running an organization, however small, and being responsible for its life and work, is of enormous value. Naturally, not all clubs succeed. Some may depend on the leadership of a particular individual or group.

Clubs rise and fall, are revived and fold up again. But this is part of the point. The club will not survive, like some school subjects, just because it is there and always has been. It will survive because it is relevant, exciting, important and above all fun to at least some children.

A third advantage of the club is that it is not classified by age or streamed by ability. It is open to members of all ages and all abilities. In a school with rigid divisions by ability the out of school activities may be the only places where children can meet and cooperate as equals without the dreariness of pre-packed academic labels. This means that their members learn not only about the club's topic but, more important, about each other. They come to understand and respect qualities, talents and skills which are different from their own, to tolerate differences, to make the most of what is available. It is not only in Cabinet committees and boards of great industries that the brilliant are assisted by the common sense judgment of the colleague of quite modest ability.

To teachers, perhaps the great virtue of the clubs is that they can meet children out of the formal atmosphere of the classroom. However free a school's methods may be, there is something necessarily formal in the relationship between a teacher and his classes. This is partly due to the fact that the class is a class—a group of thirty pupils or more. The club can be very much more a collection of individuals. So children and teachers often behave quite differently towards each other in the relaxed relationships which it makes possible.

A teacher may get to know much more about a child's thought processes, emotional sympathies and prejudices. A child may come to understand the hitherto mysterious priorities of teachers. One headmistress has said, in this context, that only when the relationship between teacher and pupil is confident and uninhibited, can teachers reach their full stature in their profession. Clearly these out of school activities are not just peripheral. Their influence can reach into the classroom and into the whole life of the school community and its members.

CHAPTER THIRTEEN

Teachers

This book so far has been about the organization of schools and what is taught in them. There will be many educators who will object that it has taken so long to get to a discussion of the teachers who work there. So one must say at once, what is true, that the quality of education depends upon the quality of teachers. One must add, what is also true, that the quality of the teaching profession has been rising steadily and constantly. So have the demands which are made upon it.

In the first place, the world is changing very fast. This means that fields of study are constantly changing too. It will no longer do, as it did in the past, for a teacher to repeat his old lecture notes annually from the time he leaves college to the time he retires. So teachers have the relatively new task of keeping up to date with their subjects. Second, the very activity of teaching is changing. We have seen how new approaches and methods are invading every area of the curriculum. This means that teachers cannot rely upon the skills that have served them well enough in the past. They have to learn new ones and adapt the old. This too calls for constant work and thought.

Third, the new approaches encourage an independent and sceptical attitude in pupils. This means that the whole relationship between teacher and taught has changed. The very fact that a teacher is much less often standing, like a lecturer, in front of a class and much more helping, tactfully and unobtrusively, in a cooperative exercise in discovery, alters the way he and his pupils think of each other. One of the hardest things for parents (and some teachers) to understand is that we are educating children to have a quite different attitude to authority from that which was common when we ourselves were at school.

Perhaps, too, this is the place to notice the influence of popular culture on today's children and young people. A lot of parents would not dignify it with the word "culture." But a culture is what it is—in the sense both of a kind of art and of a style of living. Through all the fads and phases which pass with a speed that bewilders the elderly a simple message emerges in a number of explicit or implied injunctions: be yourself, be free, distrust authority, experience, love. . . . It is an attractive philosophy, if somewhat bland, but it tends to give adults the creeps.

There are a number of consequences of this. The first is that authority, school authority as well as any other, is no longer what it was. Authority rests ultimately on a willingness to accept it, but this willingness is no longer to be relied on. This means that the schools, like other authorities, have to win acceptance. Many teachers sense this. They regard pop culture as subversive, which in this mild way it is. Unfortunately the young people themselves are ill-equipped to sustain their scepticism. It is relatively easy for the schools to gain acceptance, through all the time-honoured tribal rites they know so well. But this simply divides the young people's lives in two. The school life and the pop life remain alien to each other, and the schools fail in their major purpose, the education of the whole person.

Pop culture also has a language of its own. It was fashionable some time ago to be rather solemn about this, and it is now fashionable to sneer at the solemnity. But that there is a specific pop language cannot be denied. This is not just a matter of jargon. It has to do with the fact that pop art is trying to say something which cannot be said in any other way. Small wonder that we middle aged parents and teachers cannot understand it. But this leaves the schools with a second problem of communication: many teachers speak in ways that their pupils literally do not understand. There has always been, together with the "generation gap", a class barrier in schools, between the largely middle class teachers and the largely working class pupils. There is now a slightly different, but equally divisive, cultural barrier.

What happens is that teachers may go on depending upon the old school virtues, of loyalty, respect, sportsmanship, "purity"—only to find them evoking no response. The children prize other virtues and may be heartless in their neglect of the old ones.

Nobody would pretend that all this makes the teachers' job any easier. It not only means that he has to regard his class, not as a captive audience, but one whose interest has to be caught and kept, but also that there are no certainties left, of behaviour or response. The demands this makes on adaptability are enormous. And since adaptability requires confidence, the need for teachers themselves to be secure, balanced, mature and mentally tough has never been greater. What is astonishing, in some ways, is that with the great expansion of numbers entering teaching so very many of them are so very good. And if, in the general uncertainty, many teachers turn in self-defence to conservatism and assertion of authority (in general and their own) it is scarcely up to any of us spectators to sneer at them. Such advances as are made in education are, after all, made by teachers.

The general critisism that is often made of teachers is that it takes too long for new ideas to get through to them. This is partly because refresher courses and in-service training are still not common enough. What is more, teaching is a physically, emotionally and intellectually exhausting job. It occupies, indeed demands, one's whole attention. I sometimes get the impression that teachers feel about the champions of new methods rather as a man might who was sailing round Cape Horn in a howling gale and found himself approached by a boat load of nitwits screaming that he would do better with an engine. Maybe, they feel, but meanwhile we must concentrate on the matter in hand.

On the other hand, teachers are often surprisingly unaware of what is being discovered in education. Parents are often puzzled to find that they can often give very little convincing explanation for what they do, or that they seem not to be very well versed in the arguments for and against some powerful controversy, like streaming by ability or even secondary reorganization. Perhaps most of them are too little aware of the connection between social class and educational attainment, and almost none of them understand how their own expectations for pupils may affect the pupils' performance. You will hear teachers claiming that selection or streaming on the basis of their own assessments of ability is the fairest possible when all the evidence is that it is highly unsatisfactory. Indeed, the next educational battle, as reorganization becomes complete, will be about opening genuine equality of opportunity *within* the new secondary schools. And this battle will be nastier than the last because teachers will claim that it involves political or other interference with the internal affairs of schools.

In an important sense they will be right. Teaching and learning are not mechanical or impersonal activities. Education is more than facts or skills or opinions. It is at best a delicate system of personal relationships—and the freedom of teachers in their classrooms is an important recognition of this. The teacher's task is to create an atmosphere in which learning can best take place, and more and more of them believe that this implies confidence and freedom. What they would argue is that it would be hard for them to give to pupils conditions which they themselves lacked. This may be right, but it does not imply that the community has not legitimate interest in what goes on in schools. What it means is that teachers, like other public servants, must actively seek to gain the confidence of the community in what they are doing.

Be this as it may, we must now turn to see how teachers are trained for their new tasks and what support they get once they are in the schools.

How teachers are trained.

There are two main ways in which people become teachers. Most go to a college of education for a three year course and come out with a teacher's certificate. About a quarter of all the teachers in state schools have come into teaching by a different route: by going to university and getting a degree in a particular subject or group of subjects. Some of these graduate teachers have also done a year's course on teacher training, but one can still be recognized as a qualified teacher simply on the strength of having a degree. (But now graduate teachers must be trained after 1973).

A college of education is one of many kinds of institutions of higher education. Such an institution is entered at the age of 18 or so and normally requires some specified form of entry qualification. For example, universities require at least two subjects at GCE A level, and competition to get in is so strong that young people going to universities normally have very much better qualifications than those, like three A levels with high marks in each. The formal entry qualification for colleges of education is less than for universities: in fact five subjects at O level. But in practice very few young people going into the colleges have qualifications as low as those. Increasingly, individual colleges have the same minimum requirements of two A levels as universities.

There are two main kinds of colleges of education: the general and specialist. Their names are fairly self-explanatory: a specialist college concentrates on training teachers for particular subjects like domestic science (now called home economics), physical education, handicrafts, music, drama, or arts and crafts. The general colleges do not concentrate in this way, but as we shall see, the individual students normally specialise in a particular academic discipline.

The course in a college of education is made up of four main parts, which are interrelated and overlap. First, there is the student's own personal education. It ought to go without saying that teachers should be educated people. Colleges differ in what they offer here, but in most of them the student chooses one or two subjects and studies them to as high an academic level as he can. Since he starts at A level or a little below he may take his academic subjects to something like the standard of a pass degree.

The second group of topics in the course can be described under the general heading of study of education. This means that the students come to understand children and particularly how they grow and develop. They learn how children think, feel and learn as they grow up. They also study society and its effects upon education. A teacher has to know the context in which education takes place, has to understand the social pressures which are bearing upon his pupils and their homes. The "education" part of the course includes historical, sociological, psychological and philosophical studies.

The third element in the course is concerned with the act of teaching itself. The students learn about teaching methods and the theoretical basis of teaching particular subjects and skills. And this leads naturally to the fourth element—which consists of practical work in schools. Colleges differ in the amount of time they devote to this, which many students regard as the most useful and necessary, and some offer as little as four weeks a year. When a student from college goes into a school, he first observes children in the classroom and elsewhere. Then he gradually is asked to take lessons of his own, and in those schools where this teaching practice is well organized he may come to carry a limited but serious responsibility for the work of a group or class. Teaching practice is not confined to one particular kind of school, but the object is to give students the chance to experience as many kinds as possible. Some students are also encouraged to do some experimental or research work in the year at college.

The object of the college of education course is to turn out adaptable teachers, but it is normal for the course to be directed towards either primary or secondary teaching. Many courses try to get the best of both worlds by concentrating on the age range covered by the junior schools and the lower forms of secondary schools.

The most common objections to the training of teachers are: first, that the course is too theoretical and too little related to the experience the students meet when they become teachers; second, that it is bad for teachers to be trained in isolation from students of other subjects and professions; third, that the intellectual level of many of the courses is too low, and fourth, that a teacher's career is isolated from "real life" by the fact of his coming from school (as a pupil) to college and back to school again (as a teacher). Many people working in colleges of education accept the force of these criticisms.

On the other hand it must be said that the colleges have played a significant part in making possible the spread of new methods in the schools. It is not too much to say that the most adventurous teachers have normally been those trained in the colleges rather than those coming through universities. This is especially true of primary schools, but holds good in secondary schools too. It may be that some of the air of unreality about college courses which students complain of arises because the colleges are trying to change educational practice which teachers in the schools are seeking to preserve.

The other main source of supply for teaching is the universities. Normally a degree course lasts three or four years. At the end of this time a young man or woman entering teaching may do so directly or may take a year's course of training. The elements of the training course are very similar to those of the three-year course in a college of education, except that the personal education of the student is assumed to have been taken care of by the previous degree course. The rewards for graduates are high. A teacher with an honours degree gets £100 a year more than one without for the rest of his career; a teacher with a good honours degree gets £220 a year more.

It is a permanent question whether there are enough teachers for the schools. In one sense there probably are. The size of classes in secondary schools is slowly falling, and the raising of the school leaving age will not interrupt this decline for very long. Nothing is perfect, and improvement is always possible, but it does not look as though the development of the new secondary schools is threatened by an overall shortage of staff. But things are not so happy if one looks at the various kinds of teachers available. The trouble here is that the changes in the schools are creating greater demands. A secondary system which has a selection at 11 plus for various kinds of schools meant in practice that specialist teachers with degrees in particular disciplines were concentrated in the grammar schools. In fact three quarters of the teachers in grammar schools have degrees, whereas only one in five teachers in secondary modern schools do so. It is certainly not the case that teachers with degrees, or even good degrees, are the best teachers. Indeed we have seen that they might be among the more tradition-alist and suspicious of change. But in so far as a degree represents a level of educational attainment in a particular subject, it measures the level of skill available. It is quite clear that if we are to offer the same kinds of opportunity to all children as has been commonly available in grammar schools, we shall need very many more teachers with high specialist skills. At the very least, we shall need to see that all schools are staffed as well as existing comprehensive schools, two-thirds of whose teachers are graduates. This sort of demand reveals a very serious shortage indeed of teachers of science and mathematics. It may be that the colleges of education will be able to meet part of the demand by producing trained teachers with a high level of achievement in these subjects. But it is by no means clear that they can, and there is a serious fear that the teaching of science and mathematics in the new secondary schools will quite simply break down.

The Schools Council.

One of the most obvious facts about British teachers is their freedom. We have seen, in Chapter One, how the Department of Education and Science does not own or run the schools. Nor is it the business of the Department to lay down what should be taught, or how. It is the local education authorities which own and maintain schools.

But they do not lay down what should be taught either. They may make regulations, for example about the circumstances under which pupils may be caned, but broadly speaking an authority does not interfere with what goes on inside schools. Technically, this is a matter for the governors of a school. Governors are appointed by the local authority it is true (though there are some categories of school in which the local authority governors are in a minority) and they often reflect the political composition of the local authority. But the authority does not use governors as a way of influencing syllabuses or teaching methods. What the governors do in practice is to leave matters like this to the headmaster and his staff. A similar freedom exists within schools. A headmaster may have his own views about teaching methods and the like, and he may seek to gather round him a staff who broadly agree with him. The broad plan of work in any particular subject or group of subjects may be in the hands of a senior teacher in that subject who may be called a head of department. He and all the subject teachers may certainly consult about what ground should be covered and the way certain topics might be tackled. But it is very rare indeed for either a head teacher or a head of department to intervene in the teaching of any individual member of staff, and once a teacher faces a class, what happens is in practice almost entirely up to him.

Parents who meet this freedom for teachers for the first time are often puzzled by it. They feel that there should be somewhere, or from someone, a directive about what should be taught. They might argue that a national education system should be expected to take all its pupils through more or less the same curriculum. In a broad sense it does. The central core of any school curriculum is based upon the same group of subjects. But what is actually taught may vary widely from one school to another. Indeed we have seen throughout this book how not only the methods of teaching and the educational approach may vary, but also how the very subject matter of a course may be quite different from one school to another, and even within a single school.

There is, however, one constraint under which teachers and schools work which ensures that standards and even curricula are roughly comparable: this is the system of public examinations. These, the General Certificate of Education and the Certificate of Secondary Education, are described in Chapter Eleven. There are many examining boards, and so schools have a choice of the kind of examination they might take. Nevertheless, the freedom of teachers to teach what they like and how they like is handicapped by the structure of examinations even though there is no formal compulsion.

It was indeed partly this feeling that teachers were at the mercy of external examinations that led to the setting up of a body called the Schools Council for the Curriculum and Examinations. This body, which is known as the Schools Council for short, has as its object to uphold the principle that each school should have the fullest possible measure of responsibility for its own work, with its own curriculum and teaching methods based on the needs of its own pupils and evolved by its own staff. The idea is that this object is best achieved through the cooperation of all those who have to do with curricula and examinations. One of the most important facts about the Council is that most of its members represent teachers in schools, either through their organizations or as individuals. The other members are representatives of local authorities, the churches, the examining boards, the Department of Education and Science and so on. What the Council does is to sponsor and encourage research into the educational needs of pupils and the community and the way these can best be met by the curriculum. It has also taken over the functions of the Secondary School Examination Council which had co-ordinated the work of the GCE Boards. It operates through a rather elaborate structure of policy and executive committees. There are sub-committees for example on primary education, preparing for raising the school leaving age and the sixth form. There are CSE and GCE committees, and there are sixteen committees for particular subjects. In all of these teachers have a majority. The Council now has a permanent staff of about ninety people, and its offices are at 160 Great Portland Street, London W.1. It spends about £1¼m a year.

In its first five years or so, the Council has had an important effect in developing new kinds of courses and in spreading information about these and others in the schools. One of the ways in which it does this is by the creation of "teachers' centres" in which teachers can meet to develop the new ideas in the light of the council's publications, national development projects and other sorts of information. There are perhaps 250 such centres spread throughout the country. Many of them house extensive libraries of books and records. Others have well equipped laboratories. Most of them offer courses, seminars, workshops and practice in new methods. The council also employs field officers, most of whom are head teachers who have experience of curriculum changes. These officers visit schools and teachers' centres to spread information and ideas. There is also a whole heap of publications put out by the council. Most numerous are the examinations bulletins which give the results of the trials of new experimental examinations. As yet there are not so many curriculum bulletins, which set out the state of innovation and experiment at the time of publication, but there are numbers of what are called working papers. These are pamphlets whose purpose is to stimulate thought and discussion. One of the most important consequences of research sponsored by the council is the publication *Young School Leavers*, the report of an enquiry carried out for the council by the Government Social Survey, which has been mentioned many times in the course of this book.

What happens when the Council launches a development project? Let us imagine that a committee wishes to study science for the school leaver. It first of all tries to define the needs of pupils and society as a whole, and it does this partly through a survey of the existing aims and practices. This survey also reveals some of the most effective ways in which teachers are already fulfilling some of their own objectives. Even this, the first, stage can be a help to teachers in showing which of their aims are of most central interest and importance, in enabling teachers to look at their own methods of work in the light of the practice of others, and in revealing what else needs to be done in the development of new materials.

In the second stage of the project, the Council commissions a team of teachers and professional researchers, designers and others to devise new materials which seem to be needed. The teams are usually based on a university or college of education and the materials may include teachers' guides, text books, pictures, charts, films, film strips and teachers' aids of all kinds. When all this is ready, the new materials are tried in selected schools. This trial itself may alter the practice of teachers in the schools selected, because after all the development of new materials almost always stems from new approaches to learning and teaching. Often the teachers in the selected schools go on explanatory courses. It is at this stage that the effectiveness of the new materials is tried out.

If all goes well, the new methods and materials go into general publication, there may be a council publication together with conferences and courses for teachers. And when all this is done, the council may set up a team to follow the results of the new materials once they are in general use—and presumably after a period of time the whole process of change and innovation begins again.

The Inspectors.

New ideas and methods are also passed to the schools by Her Majesties Inspectors (HMIs) and local inspectors. HMIs are normally former teachers. They value and emphasize their independent status, though they are attached to the Department of Education and Science. They are headed by a senior chief inspector, and below him are six chief inspectors each responsible for one branch of education, like secondary education, the training of teachers or educational developments. Staff inspectors may be responsible for particular school subjects or for detailed aspects of the education service. For inspection, the country is divided into divisions, and each division into districts, each with an inspector. Each local authority has its own inspectors, organisers and advisers whose jobs roughly correspond with those of the HMIs.

The most obvious thing the inspectors do is to inspect: their work sprang from early attempts to see that standards were maintained, and this is still part of their job. They may do it either singly or by a full inspection in which a group of them stay in a school for several days. But inspectors do not give orders. Their job is to report, with praise or blame, and to advise. It is for the local authorities and the schools to decide what to do as a result of a report. But more than ever, the HMIs see their role much more in terms of advice than of inspection. They interpret Government policy, and in particular they gather from their visits to schools and colleges a vast knowledge of new studies, methods and techniques, and this they pass on to other teachers and other schools. Teachers sometimes feel that the inspectors, like the colleges of education, are a little remote from the reality of the classroom. On the other hand, few teachers make really intelligent use of the inspectorate and the skill and experience they offer. Inspectors also run short courses for teachers, produce pamphlets and sit on all manner of boards and committees at which policy and practice are discussed.

Central Advisory Councils.

The inspectors are quite good at making new ideas familiar to large numbers of teachers. There is also a device for turning new ideas into the accepted wisdom. This is the device of the Central Advisory Councils for Education (there is one for England and one for Wales). These bodies are set up by law to advise the Secretary of State for

Education and Science. They can themselves decide what they wish to give advice on, but in practice they have considered and reported on topics chosen for them by the Secretary of State. Their reports, which come to be known by the name of the chairmen at the time, have included the Crowther Report (on 15 to 18 year olds) the Newsom Report (on 13 to 16 year olds of average and below average ability) and the Plowden Report (on primary schools). You might think that these reports to the Secretary of State might have little interest for teachers, but in fact what the councils do is to survey the whole field concerning them at the time and advise absolutely everybody: Secretary of State, local authorities, inspectors, teachers, parents and so on. In doing so they conduct surveys and inquiries and they also do what is quaintly called "taking evidence"—what this means is that they read or listen to the opinions of anyone who offers them. The bulk of this opinion is submitted by professional bodies and associations, but some of it comes from individuals. The Councils themselves are composed of intelligent and respectable people, so what they normally conclude from all their "evidence" and surveys is what is generally accepted to be the enlightened and progressive opinion. You never get anything very startling in the Council's reports: what they do is to stake out the frontiers of *acceptable* advance. This stops practice in the schools from slipping backwards, and it makes enlightenment orthodox—but already there are plenty of ideas about in the schools which are far in advance of what the Council recommended. But they have to wait for the next Council!

As you would expect, there is quite a lot in the Newsom report about new ideas for the curriculum and teaching methods in secondary schools, rather less in the Crowther report. But there are two oddities about the Central Advisory Council. The first is that it has never specifically advised, or been asked to advise on the arguments for selective or comprehensive secondary education. On the topic which has caused the most educational and public controversy since the war the Council has been silent. The second oddity springs from this: the Council has never advised on the powerful organizational and curricular problems which face large secondary schools with pupils of all kinds and levels of ability. It is certain, however, that an inquiry of this kind is urgently needed.

CHAPTER FOURTEEN

After school

Most pupils and their parents see school as a preparation for adult life, and as children grow up they come more and more to wonder what they are going to do after leaving school. Parents' interest in this may vary; some may be anxious that their sons and daughters should leave school as soon as possible in order to contribute to the family budget. These parents need the most convincing of the value of any additional education, and schools are often hard put to persuade them. Half the children of England leave school at the earliest possible opportunity. Other parents may see the vocational problem in a different way. They may think in terms of a career or profession and they will seek to know what formal qualifications are necessary to follow it. They will normally expect their sons and daughters to stay at school and then at college, for as long as is necessary to become a teacher, doctor, architect or whatever it is. This is not the place to enter into a long description of the opportunities available after school. But a book like this would be incomplete unless it indicated, however roughly, the connection between school and adult life, and showed some of the ways in which the schools prepare their pupils for it.

Let us start with the largest group of children, those who will leave as soon as they are legally entitled to do so. At present this is the leaving date after they have reached the age of 15: there are two leaving dates a year at Easter and Summer. After 1972 the age will be 16, which means that children who entered secondary schools in September 1968 will remain for a five-year course, leaving in 1973. A lot of people have been dissatisfied by the fact that there have been two leaving dates in the last compulsory year of school. Teachers in particular feel that this makes it impossible to have a full four-year course and argue that losing half one's pupils in the middle of the last year means an incomplete education for those who leave and a lowered morale for those who stay. The objection to a single date is industrial rather than educational: it is thought that it would be difficult to find jobs for all those school leavers if they came on to the labour market at once. The balance of opinion is moving towards a single leaving date; but the question has now become bound up with raising the age. In fact the Secretary of State for Education and Science has recently decided to raise the age and keep two leaving dates.

Whatever the outcome, and whether the leaving age is 15 or 16, the experience of children leaving at the earliest opportunity will be much the same. They will of course have had a certain amount of guidance, probably largely informal, from their teachers about the kinds of jobs that may be available to them. This advice is formalized, during their last year at school, through the work of the Youth Employment Service. The provision of a national youth employment service is the responsibility of the Central Youth Employment Executive which is a partnership of representatives of the Department of Employment and Productivity, the Department of Education and Science and the Scottish Education Department, but the service is operated either by the local education authority or by the DEP through its local office. The local youth employment bureau is run by a youth employment officer assisted by one or more other officers. In most of the schools the youth employment officer probably gives a general talk to school leavers at the beginning of their last year on the kinds of jobs which are likely to be available. He may talk about the general state of the labour market locally, either warning the youngsters that they may have to travel in order to find jobs or assuring them that local factories or offices are crying out for labour. This general talk may be followed up by other talks about particular kinds of jobs— in engineering, say, or nursing. And of course the talks will include information about what qualifications, if any, are necessary for entering these jobs. The next thing the youth employment officer does is to arrange for any pupil who wishes to have an interview with him or one of his officers. These interviews may take place during the day at school, but normally teachers are not present. The youth employment officer will have before him the pupil's confidential reports about health, ability, educational performance and aptitudes, and what he will try to do is to suggest suitable jobs in which he knows there are vacancies. This interview is an important one for a pupil, and parents can be present if they and he wish it. Few people would claim that the arrangements are ideal. The youngsters themselves may have little idea how to conduct the interview and may find themselves accepting proposals which they are not happy with. The youth employment officer is of course used to this and does his best to avoid it, but the service is understaffed and the officer may simply not have time to pay the kind of attention that is necessary. He is also beset by the conflicting claims of the school leaver and of local industry. Put another way, he may come to form one view of the aptitudes and capacities of the boy or girl in front of him, yet know that the jobs actually available demand something different or more limited. The best officers try to resist being merely an employment agency or placement service, but time very often is against them.

Probably about a third of all children leaving school get their first job through the Youth Employment Service, and the interest of the service does not stop there. The youth employment officer as a matter of routine invites boys and girls to come back after they have been in their jobs for some time to tell him how they are getting on, and he may often arrange "open evenings" to encourage them to do so. If the first job is unsatisfactory, he will try to find another.

Some schools themselves back up the work of the Youth Employment Service in a more informal way. In many schools there is a "careers teacher", a member of staff who is responsible for knowing about employment and careers and for finding out if he does not know. Sometimes this job is performed in a rather sketchy manner, but careers teachers themselves are beginning to agitate for a chance to do a better job. They may, for example, get a separate room set aside for careers literature and other material, and this may sometimes be attached to the school library. Some very fortunate careers teachers do a little less teaching than their colleagues on the staff in order that they can spend the time with pupils and in preparation.

Some schools make a point of arranging visits for their older children to some of the larger local firms, so that the children can get some idea of what the world of work is really like. These visits can in some cases be quite elaborate, their purpose more than simply careers advice. The visits may be as long as a week or a fortnight, and the pupils may get some experience of work rather than just observing it. None of this sort of experiences is very well developed yet in this country (as it is in, say, Sweden or the United States) but parents can expect it to be more common as schools increasingly try to relate what they are doing to adult life.

Other schools may try to begin the process of thinking about careers rather earlier than the last year at school, and may try to involve parents in the discussions. One comprehensive school, for example, has what it calls a "careers convention" towards the end of the third year at school when the children are around 14. Of course the school does not try to get pupils to settle for particular jobs at this early stage, but it does involve them in thinking about their courses in terms which are related to the future. The careers convention resembles one of those large shows at Earls Court. The school hall is filled with tables each manned by specialists in particular ranges of subjects: engineering, apprenticeships, banking and insurance, local government, teaching, nursing, the armed services and so on. The children and their parents are invited to come to the convention and many do so. At the beginning of the evening the older children can make for the specialists at their tables. The third year pupils, for whom the

evening is specifically intended, begin by hearing a talk
from the head teacher on the opportunities available at the
school, which are extremely varied, and how the pupils
and their parents might begin thinking about choosing
between them. In particular, the head teacher is likely to
emphasize the value of staying on for extra courses and
qualifications at school. After this the pupils and their
parents can go into the main convention, talk to the
specialists available and pick up any literature that they
may need. The evening rarely ends before midnight. At
this school the evening is followed up in a most elaborate
way by further discussions with teachers at which the
aptitudes and ability of the pupils, all docketted and cross-
referenced on record cards, are taken into account.

Increasingly, teachers are being prepared or are training
themselves for careers work. For example, some courses in
colleges of education have options in training for it, and
there are in-service courses organised nationally and
regionally for careers teachers. This move towards increased training is reflected in the schools themselves, where
careers work may often become a part of curriculum
development. More and more schools provide periods in the
time-table, sometimes in the third year and more frequently for fourth formers. Such periods of education are
usually supported by individual guidance and counselling.
In some schools the pupils may get time to go to the local
college of further education to look at the courses available,
and a few local authorities provide short residential
courses on careers for school leavers. The programme of
careers guidance in a school of this kind is quoted at the
end of this chapter. (See page 163).

Even for those children who leave school as soon as they
can, education need not end entirely. Many of them, of
course, will go into jobs which require no qualifications
and demand very little training. But others will have to train
specifically: shorthand typists are a good example. Some
young workers find that their jobs involve a good deal of
further education. Apprentices, in particular, will find
themselves spending a day, and perhaps an evening a week

in classes in technical colleges. Most youngsters who get any education at all get it part time in colleges of this sort. The colleges have a variety of names: technical college, college of technology, college of further education, college of commerce, colleges and institutes of agriculture, colleges of art, and so on. There is an enormous variety of institutions of this kind, and a college may be very much less specialised than its name implies: plenty of people take A levels in English and other non-technical subjects at "technical" colleges. Other youngsters may discover the importance of education and qualifications only after leaving school, though it is the job of the schools to see that as few as possible do this, and again it is the further education college that will most likely accommodate them. One of the most important things a school can do for its leavers is to make them aware of the great range of opportunity that is available.

For example, many people do not seem to realise that there is a route to the very highest qualifications open to those who leave school early. A boy showing high ability on a craft apprenticeship course may be urged to transfer to another course leading to the ordinary national certificate (ONC). These certificates, together with those at the higher level (HNC) have had a profound influence in the development of higher education outside the universities. They are awarded by joint committees of the Department of Education and Science and the relevant professional institution (the Institution of Electrical Engineers, for example) on the basis of course work and examinations of the colleges assessed by persons appointed by the joint committees (in a way that foreshadowed the principle underlying CSE, mode three). The standard reached at ONC is comparable with that of A level, and the certificate is increasingly accepted as the equivalent of A level for entry to university and other degree courses. A boy who is successful at ONC may thus go on to a university or take a degree at a technical college not unlike that at which he took his ONC, except that it would specialise more in higher level work. He might alternatively go on to take HNC, although in some areas, notably engineering, it is becoming less popular partly because the degree of exemption accorded to it by certain professional institutions has been reduced.

The important fact about the ONC is that it is taken after a part time course. (There is an ordinary national diploma, OND, taken after a full time course, but many fewer take it.) This means that a youngster who has left school and goes to work can continue his education while he is working. The ONC course, indeed, is likely to be a vocational one, related to the job he is doing or preparing him for a better one. This aspect of it has always made it attractive to the working class youngster who cannot—or whose parents cannot—be persuaded of the value of continued academic studies.

There are some young people who, although prepared to carry on in fulltime education do not wish, for one reason or another, to do so in school. These constitute a minority, but an important one, since they might well be lost to full-time education were it not for the fact that appropriate opportunities exist for them in colleges of further education. They enrole for a wide variety of full-time courses, including GCE, courses at both O and A level. Some 26,000 are taking O level courses and 23,000 A levels. Many more are taking full-time courses of the City and Guilds type, of both a craft and a technician nature. The ordinary national diploma courses are either full-time or sandwich and are taken by some 12,000 students.

Perhaps most schools are still largely ignorant of these possibilities in technical education and many of those who know about them tend to sneer at them. It is, for example, entirely common for school speech days to refer to A level success, entrants to universities and training colleges and degree successes of old pupils, yet never even to allude to entrants to technical colleges or success at ONC and HNC or in some other technical qualification. This ignorance and superciliousness are particularly reprehensible now that there is a national body responsible for the award of degrees in non-university institutions. It is the Council for National Academic Awards (CNAA) and there are already more people studying for its degrees than in any university except London. The range of degree studies available is very wide, and is growing wider. Many of the CNAA courses are based on the "sandwich" principle. A sandwich course is an integrated course in which periods of academic education in college alternate with periods of practical training in industry. It was introduced first in engineering and other technologies but is now spreading to social studies, economics, mathematics and so on.

Clearly the work of the technical colleges is extremely varied. They may offer anything from hairdressing to research degrees, by all methods of study—full-time, "sandwich", part-time, day release and so on. They attract students of all ages, from 15 or 16 to 25 and even much older. The colleges themselves have no formal entry requirements (though particular courses may have) and thus a student who finds a course too much for him may transfer to another less demanding one. Equally, a student who shows promise on one lower level course may be enticed onto a more advanced one. The colleges offer all types of courses, too, from academic ones leading to the GCE or degrees to professional and vocational education concerned with training for particular jobs and careers. It is fair to say, however, that the colleges' distinctive traditions are in professional and vocational education. Equally, although they do a great deal of research, often for local industry, they are mainly teaching rather than research institutions. They have traditionally responded to any demand for education, whether from students who want particular kinds of courses or from industry requiring the education associated with training for specific jobs. It would be right to add, too, that the quality of staff, equipment and accommodation can also be pretty variable, but students do have an assurance of standards (often higher than some university departments could conveniently reach) in those courses moderated by the CNAA and other bodies like those responsible for national certificates.

Although it is true that any one college may offer work of all levels, an attempt has been made to rationalise the distribution of courses by grouping colleges according to the level of their work. The majority of the colleges, some 300, concentrate mainly, and possibly entirely, on work at or below ONC level, including City and Guilds courses, GCE O and A level and Royal Society of Arts courses. The majority of their work is part-time day or part-time evening although many of them offer some courses on a full-time basis. There are some 160 colleges which offer much the same range of courses, but augmented by certain advanced ones, notably higher national certificates, advanced craft courses and the like. A few of them even offer degree courses although only three provide for the CNAA degree. Some two dozen other establishments have little lower level work and concentrate on work at or above the HNC level. From the colleges doing advanced work some 60 have been selected to be developed into 30 polytechnics. These will be the apex of a second sector of higher education which, with its own traditions and its own opportunities will be developed alongside the universities. They will be comprehensive academic communities for students at all levels of higher education. They will offer courses of degree level and just below to the kinds of student traditionally accommodated in the technical colleges. Only a few polytechnics have so far been formally designated, but many of them have been "approved", and will be designated once they have fulfilled a number of conditions laid down by the Secretary of State.

The other, major, route to higher education has been through the sixth forms of the schools, via A level to universities and colleges of education. The latter have already been described fully in the chapter on teachers. Normally, people go to training college after getting at least five O levels and probably an A level or two.

For university, candidates normally need five or more GCE passes including two or more at A level. The competition for entry is getting keener, partly through the success of the schools in mitigating the effects of selection at 11 plus. More and more young people are staying on and getting the GCE results which were earlier thought likely only from a small "academic" minority. This has meant, however, that universities have been demanding more than their formal minimum entry qualifications: in some three A levels with high gradings are necessary. And individual departments of universities may have their own particular requirements.

All this means that university students are almost all aged 18 to 21 or 22 and have arrived there through the sixth forms. There are some who have taken or retaken O and A levels at technical colleges, and a few (particularly in the technological universities) who have entered through ONC. The courses they follow are pretty well all full time (though, again, the technological universities have sandwich courses) and lead after three or four years to the hallmark of an academic education—a university degree. Some students stay on at university to do a second, higher degree too.

What characterises the universities is their concern for "knowledge for its own sake". They are centres of learning, giving the same priority to research as to teaching students, and there are large areas of their work which are in no way concerned with professional or vocational education—and even ostensibly vocational courses like law, theology or medicine very often require further practical experience before final qualification. They describe their purpose as preserving, extending and disseminating knowledge. Perhaps because they are thought to be remote from practical affairs, perhaps because of their limited access points, the universities have not been very successful in attracting working class students. Only a quarter of university students have working class fathers—the same proportion as in 1928.

There is clearly a whole range of opportunity open to youngsters after they leave school, and it is part of the schools' job to introduce them to it and make it possible for them to take some of the opportunities up. Some of the new developments in schools, like the Certificate of Secondary Education, are designed to open these opportunities to more children. Other innovations, like extended visits to factories, shops and offices, are meant to link school with the world of work. And we have seen that there are still places where the schools still have some way to go in making information readily available: there is still too little knowledge of and co-operation with the whole field of further education. There are two major routes to the highest qualifications. One lies through the academic institutions: school, A levels and university. The other lies through work and part-time education in technical colleges, through ONC and CNAA degrees. It should be noted that these two routes are not mutually exclusive. Increasing numbers of sixth formers go to CNAA degree courses in colleges and not to universities. Also, as mentioned earlier, many students with good ONCs progress, not necessarily to CNAA courses in colleges, but possibly to degree courses in universities. The new schools have the task of showing their pupils the vast range of appropriate courses and offering the means to embark upon them.

Chaucer Comprehensive School, Sheffield.

Programme of Vocational Guidance.

During the first two years each class has ONE period per week with a form teacher. These are generally supervised by the Year Tutors and a scheme of work is provided by the Head of the Department.

In the third, fourth and fifth years, each form has a period with either a Year Tutor or the Head of the Department. During the fourth and fifth years, the Youth Employment Officers assist in the careers lessons. A careers convention is held each year in the school.

AUTUMN TERM

SIXTH FORM—Interviews with Youth Employment Officer and Head of Vocational Guidance Dept., followed by

interviews with Head of Department and Sixth Form
Master regarding applications to Colleges and Universities.
Distribution of UCCA forms, completion, collection—
forms passed to Headmaster for Head's report. Central
Careers Convention during Christmas holidays.

FIFTH FORM—Talks by Youth Employment Officers.
Individual interviews with Year Tutor or Head of Department. Preparation of Y.15s. Central Careers Convention
during Christmas holidays.

FOURTH FORM—Talks by Youth Employment Officers.
Individual interviews with Year Tutor or Head of Department. Careers visits throughout term. Y.15s prepared at
beginning of term. Interview with Youth Employment
Officer and member of careers department at end of term
(parents invited).

OLD STUDENTS—Coffee evening for pupils who left previous
year. Head, Senior Mistress, Careers Staff and Youth
Employment Officers present to discuss any problems
which have arisen during early months at work.

WINTER TERM

SIXTH FORM—Individual interviews over problems regarding
interviews at Colleges, Universities etc. Interviews with
Youth Employment Officer of pupils wishing to take up
employment at end of year. Careers visits during Easter
holidays.

FIFTH FORM—Continue individual interviews with careers
staff. Interviews with Youth Employment Officers and
careers staff for pupils leaving school at mid-summer.
Completion of Estimation of Exam. Performance forms.
Careers visits during Easter holidays.

FOURTH FORM—Further talks by Youth Employment

Officers. Continue individual interviews with careers staff and preparation of Y.15s for midsummer leavers. Placing of Easter leavers by Youth Employment Officers. Distribution of National Insurance Cards and final placing check by Youth Employment Officers. Continue programme of visits. Completion of testimonials for Easter leavers. Boys to have work experience course at College of Further Education.

SUMMER TERM

SIXTH FORM—Talk to Lower Sixth on "Application Procedure for Colleges and Universities" (Head of Dept., and Youth Employment Officers). Placing of midsummer leavers. Final checking of pupils hoping to go to College or University. After A level results, interviewing of pupils who have problems about University entrance. Group discussions on professional careers and higher education.

FIFTH FORM—Interviews for pupils wishing to go into Sixth form (Advice regarding choice of subjects for Sixth form course). Placing of midsummer leavers by Youth Employment Officers. Series of talks and visits after O level exams have ended to help pupils in the transition from school to work. Series of careers visits for those entering 6th Form professional careers. Completion of testimonials forms. Final placing. Conference with Youth Employment Officers.

FOURTH FORM—Continue programme of visits. Interviews at beginning of term with Youth Employment Officers and Careers Staff for midsummer leavers. Placing of midsummer leavers by Youth Employment Officers. Final placing conference and distribution of Insurance Cards. Preparation of Testimonials.

THIRD FORM—Parents evening to explain arrangements for choosing subjects to be studied in Fourth and Fifth forms

(Head of Dept., Year Tutor and Youth Employment Officers present to give advice on importance and relevance of certain subject choices). Year Tutors to supervise distribution and collection of forms. Conference of Deputy Head, Head of Department and Year Tutor to discuss individual choices before completion of time table.

CHAPTER FIFTEEN

The pace of change

Over the next few years secondary education in England and Wales will become increasingly comprehensive. But how quickly? Cynics remember that it took a quarter of a century for the last educational reorganisation (giving us the primary and secondary schools we have today) to be completed. Are things likely to be more or less sluggish this time?

Educational change depends upon two main kinds of provision, of teachers and of buildings. The supply of teachers has already been covered in Chapter Thirteen: we have seen that there will be difficulties, particularly in science and mathematics, but these are more likely to affect the quality of the education provided than the speed of change. The major constraint is that of buildings. Secondary reorganisation has coincided with a period of economic difficulty, so there have quite simply been no extra resources available. Local authorities have largely had to do the best they can within the normal building programmes. Indeed the publication, in Circular 10/65, of six acceptable methods of reorganising was a recognition by the Government that change would have to take place largely in existing buildings. Whatever might be said for or against the sixth form colleges or two tier arrangements described in Chapter One, a local authority is likely to adopt them, not for abstract educational reasons but for solidly practical ones. How, in short, can one accommodate the new kinds of schools and the new principles of education in the buildings which happen to be available? It is not that these buildings are necessarily very old: we have seen how three quarters of the children in secondary schools are in places provided since the war. But buildings put up as grammar schools or secondary modern schools may not be suitable as comprehensives. They may lack the necessary range of specialist rooms and equipment. Above all, they may be too small.

So an education committee and its officers have to show some ingenuity if they are to reorganise satisfactorily. Above all, they have to be flexible, and this can lead to wide variations in the solutions evolved, not only between local authorities but within the areas of individual ones. It is not, of course, that the authorities have no resources for building in general. The total school building programme these days is running at over £170m. a year, which is scarcely peanuts, and a third of that is for major building for secondary schools. This major programme is for two main purposes, called "basic needs" and "improvement". The latter is self explanatory: money for improvement is used to rebuild, remodel or extend existing schools, some of which may be very old. Basic needs are the accommodation of new populations of school children. This includes both those children who are part of the increase in population as a whole and those whose parents have moved, often to new housing estates, and thus need new schools near their new homes. Since the war the bulk of the effort in school building has gone towards basic needs—or "roofs over heads" as it is less officially put. One consequence of this is that the older centres of large cities, from which populations are moving out, have been starved of new school building, and this deficiency has scarcely been made up by recent special measures for schools in decaying areas. On the other hand, building a new school on a new housing estate may itself be thought of partly as improvement, as it will take in children who have moved from the old city centres. But people who are puzzled to notice that the pleasanter counties or suburbs near large cities have bigger building programmes than the older industrial towns can find the answer in the policy for giving priority to the housing of new school populations.

As well as the major building programmes there is

another, smaller one for the financing of "minor works". These are building projects costing less than £20,000, and they were introduced partly to compensate the slum schools in town centres. For £20,000 you can civilise the lavatories, build some extra classrooms or specialist rooms or do some conversion.

And on top of all this there are special building programmes for special purposes. The largest, and most recent, of these is the money being spent between 1970 and 1973 to accommodate the extra children who will be staying at school after the raising of the school leaving age in 1972. This amounts to well over £100m.

All these overall programmes are decided by the Department of Education and Science after negotiations with the Treasury. They are announced in advance and the local authorities are asked to submit their proposals for spending their shares of it. The proposals are scrutinised by the Department which approves (or rejects) each project individually. Within the total amount of money available, the local authority suggests in the first instance where the money should be spent, but the final decision rests with the Department.

A building programme like this leaves the local authorities with a good deal of flexibility, and in particular the various purposes of the school building programme may get inextricably mixed up together. For example, an authority might decide that the time has come to build a new secondary school for a new housing estate. Looking at the total programme and going on previous experience of its likely share of it, the authority might conclude that a first instalment should go ahead. But the chief officer might suggest using some of the money for raising the school leaving age to build a second instalment at the same time. But then a member of the committee might object that there is already a small secondary school quite near, which could equally well be extended. Whereupon another member might remind his colleagues that they have been trying for years to rebuild a local primary school whose building dates from Victorian times and has been recommended for demolition. It would be no surprise if the committee in the end decided to pull down the old primary school; move the primary children into the small secondary school, after a minor works project to help the adaptation; and build a complete, entirely new and very large secondary school on the new estate to accommodate the children from the small secondary school as well as new ones coming in. And the chief officer might remind them, as a bonus, that this would make more sense anyway if a future move toward comprehensive schools made large secondary school buildings more appropriate than small ones.

Given twenty years of this kind of flexibility, it is clear that local authorities wishing to reorganise their secondary schools are unlikely to be daunted by the lack of a specific building programme for doing so. The process may take longer, but there is no doubt that it can happen in the end. For their part, Ministers have said that they will not approve new building projects which are incompatible with reorganisation. This means, broadly, that they will not accept proposals for small schools or for separate grammar schools; the emphasis is on extending existing schools as well as establishing new ones. This has led to a certain amount of argument with some authorities, notably Surrey and later Birmingham, because the authorities claimed that Ministers were holding up necessary building in order to force them into reorganising. Ministers were indeed doing just that—and the fact that they were shows that even where there are few resources specifically set aside for reorganisation, much can be done within the very large building programme to which the education service is now accustomed.

What this means for local authorities is that they look at all their building needs together; primary, secondary, basic needs, improvement, raising the age, going comprehensive and so on. And they look at their likely resources: for major and minor works and for raising the age. Then they simply match the two as best they can, without sticking to rigid headings. One local authority, for example, is in effect using the money for raising the school leaving age to establish a series of middle schools and thus create a three tier comprehensive system, of primary, middle and senior schools, throughout its area. Not all authorities have been as radical as that, but most authorities go through a similar exercise.

Perhaps the best evidence for the way in which building programmes serve many purposes came when the original programme for raising the school leaving age in 1972 was postponed in the economy measures of 1968. Ministers discovered at the time that they could not postpone the whole amount—and they discovered later that a further £3.5m. had to be found to "protect" schemes of reorganisation which would otherwise be lost. This latter sum is in fact the amount which can be said to have been specifically set aside for "going comprehensive".

What has generally happened in planning a scheme of reorganisation is this. A local education authority, having received Circular 10/65 from the Department of Education and Science, would deal with it at its next council meeting. Normally things were fairly formal at that stage and the circular was remitted to the education committee, with whatever comment or instruction the council thought fit. The education committee might or might not have sent it on to the secondary education sub-committee. Wherever it ended up, the circular was likely to have been the subject of a pretty long discussion, concentrating on the members' reaction to the principle of the thing, but also getting involved with a good deal of detail as people brought up individual examples or difficulties. The end of this stage came, perhaps after a number of meetings for which the officials prepared background papers, when the committee and the council decided that a plan should be prepared. (As we have seen it was possible for the education authority to baulk at the whole thing even at this point).

What usually happened then was that the chief education officer and his staff were asked to prepare an outline plan, and they might even have been given some pretty clear indication of the kind of scheme the committee or the council would eventually accept. The officers prepared estimates of the likely numbers of children in the schools for perhaps ten years or more ahead and surveyed their existing school premises and their related "catchment areas". Their task was to match the numbers to the schools in accordance with the principles of reorganisation. Very often this first plan was drawn up "in the office" and few people outside got to know much about it. But some authorities also brought in working parties composed of representatives of teachers' organisations at this stage. This helped them to gauge in advance the likely reactions of teachers, but it also recognised the professional responsibility of teachers in matters which intimately affected their work. There are many people who feel that this stage of the process could have been improved by even wider consultation, and in some authorities, the views of all kinds of organisations were invited. These representations were made somewhat "in the dark" however, since the outline of the plan was not then known.

Once the officials' plan had been presented to the education committee it became a public document and the debate began on it in earnest. This took place not only within the meetings of the local authority but outside as well. The local press probably published the proposals in full, and may have carried an interminable correspondence. The local teachers' associations met to formalise their attitude to the scheme. Local churches, which might control some of the schools, did the same. If there was a parents' body, like a local association for the advancement of state education, it may have held a series of public meetings. The local political parties will have been humming with activity and disagreement. Councillors and officials spent their time explaining, defending and converting. There may have been parents' meetings in individual schools.

The authority, of course, would try to carry as much agreement to its proposals as it could, and it might have modified some parts of them in the face of strong pressure. Some authorities, on the other hand, have been pretty stiff-necked, and this combined with thoughtlessness and haste has led to prolonged campaigns against them and even to one or two being taken through the courts. Up to a point, of course, this is the acceptable consequence of democratic administration, and people probably ought to be more astonished that the thing has gone so smoothly than worried about the occasional explosion.

After some considerable time and argument, the authority will no doubt have felt justified in asking the officers to prepare a final version of the plan—which was unlikely to differ fundamentally from the earlier one, though it might have been much changed in detail. Once the committee and the council had formally accepted it, it went off to the Secretary of State for Education and Science for his approval.

In the Department of Education and Science there is now a team of civil servants, headed by an Assistant Secretary, whose job it is to study the plans and recommend to the Secretary of State what action he should take. What they try to be certain about is that plans are consistent with Circular 10/65—that is, that they should actually abolish selection and in an acceptable way—and that the detailed proposals are reasonable and effective. Faced with a proposal for an all through 11 to 18 school accommodated in two buildings a mile apart, the civil servant might suggest that the authority give further thought to the idea of a frank, two-tier arrangement. Given proposals for parental choice, he might probe more deeply to see whether this does not involve a concealed selection process. And so on.

The Department sees and considers the plans only when they are formally submitted, but in fact a good deal of consultation has probably already gone on, often with the relevant HMIs. Chief Officers are likely to check smaller points on the telephone, or chairmen of committees may call into the Department for a long discussion. A lot is done, in other words to minimise the chances of rejection or of a prolonged haggle at the formal level. But the arguments in the locality and the consultation with the Department can go on, of course, while the formal consideration is taking place. In extreme cases Ministers may see a number of deputations.

In the end, the team of civil servants makes a recommendation, and the Secretary of State accepts or rejects the scheme—or accepts part of it and rejects others. The part Ministers play depends very much on them. The Secretary of State has four junior Ministers in his Department, and one of them, a Minister of State, has a special responsibility for schools, including reorganisation. This Minister sees all the plans at an early stage and will make a recommendation on what should be done. But Ministers differ in the extent to which they get involved. Some are content to satisfy themselves that the process of approval is running smoothly. Others take an interest in the smallest details of each scheme. Similarly, Secretaries of State can differ in the interest they devote to reorganisation: they have, after all, the whole of the rest of the education service to think about. For one Secretary of State, reorganisation may have the highest priority for his attention: another might treat it as one, no doubt important, issue among many. In other words, the approval of Ministers is no empty formality. They can set their stamp upon the speed and quality of administrative change, by being anything from an inspiration to a nuisance, like the heads of any large organisation.

If the Secretary of State accepts a scheme, the authority can go ahead, though there may still be arguments about detail and, of course, a sudden influx of new populations may cause even radical revision. In any case, the whole plan is unlikely to be put into effect immediately. It will depend not only upon new buildings but also on the need to change the function and character of some schools with as little disruption as possible. And this may take time.

But how much time? The answer to this will differ from one place to another, but it may help to show how the country as a whole is going. At present 108 local authorities have plans implemented or approved for the whole of their areas, or for part of their areas; and only 34 have no plans approved at all. Of the approved plans, 89 provide for all through schools; 41 for two tier arrangements; 47 for middle schools; and 25 for sixth form colleges. (Many authorities are using more than one of these methods). In 1969, 94 out of 163 local authorities had 962 comprehensive schools in operation, or 18 per cent of all secondary schools in the country as a whole. Of the whole secondary schools population, 771,000 or 26 per cent, were in comprehensive schools.

This, then, is the pace of change. And perhaps, whether you agree with abolishing selection or not, you may feel it is too slow: every year's delay represents, after all, uncertainty and perhaps muddle in a locality. Transitional arrangements are, by their very nature, makeshift. Up to a point, the remedy is in our own hands: with more resources the job could be done more quickly, so we need a continuing lobby for educational spending. But there is a sense in which sluggishness is inevitable. Social revolutions take time. After 1944 the nation failed to redeem the promise of secondary education for all. We must not fail again.

This book has been about the new comprehensive schools and what goes on inside them. These schools have grown from the desire to end the folly and injustice of selection at 11 plus. They are spreading because most people want them to. The new subjects they offer and the new methods they use are largely welcome to parents, pupils and teachers. Of course much remains to be done, and some brave spirits are already mapping out the *next* reform. But today's changes will not be undone: they will become the basis for the next advance.

What the new schools are doing is to offer a full secondary education, not just to the relatively rich (as we did before the war) or to the relatively clever (as we tried to do after 1944) but to all children. The ways in which they do this, and their success in it, will always and rightly be matters for debate. I believe we have now given the schools a framework in which they can succeed. We are at last removing their most obvious handicaps. For this we can thank local and national politicians and administrators and innumerable researchers and publicists. That the schools

G

themselves are rising to their opportunities is due to the work and vision of their teachers and those who train and advise them. But the objects of the whole exercise, the pupils, are not just passive beneficiaries of all this attention: they too, with their parents, help to create the new secondary education. While I have been writing this book I have visited large numbers of schools. And my final impression is not so much of new buildings, unfamiliar methods, expensive equipment or smooth administration as of a whole new generation of children and young people whose maturity and ability are startlingly impressive. We are rearing a creative and critical generation. And if you doubt me, then go and see for yourself.

Reorganisation plans for maintained schools in England and Wales

Introduction

The information in this Appendix was supplied by the Department of Education and Science and relates to the position reached in January 1970 when it was prepared.

For many areas of the country it is not possible to describe in a few words all the complexities of reorganisation. Nor is it generally possible to give dates for implementation. In almost all areas the changeover to a comprehensive system must be spread over a period of years: county schools may be reorganised on a different timetable from voluntary schools: voluntary schools of one denomination may proceed on a different basis from those of another: time-tables for changeover are often dependent on the size and character of school building programmes and dates for the availability of new buildings cannot be predicted accurately.

For these reasons the information given for each local education authority area should be regarded as giving a general indication of the position reached on reorganisation. For details about proposals for individual schools or the timing of the ending of selection enquiries should be made of the local education authority.

Anglesey

All maintained secondary schools are comprehensive, having been reorganised before the issue of Circular 10/65.

Barking

A revised plan, covering county schools only, for 11–18 schools was approved in principle in November 1968. The authority are working towards complete implementation in September 1970. Proposals for Roman Catholic schools are under consideration.

Barnet

A plan was approved in July 1968 and involves a mixture of 11–18 and two tier 11–14, 14–18 schools. The plan covers the Roman Catholic and Church of England schools as well as a Jewish voluntary school. Implementation is expected to begin in 1971.

Barnsley

A plan was approved in 1966. Both county and voluntary schools are to be reorganised on a two tier 11–14, 14–18 basis. Implementation is expected to take place in 1973–74.

Barrow-in-Furness

A plan for county and voluntary aided schools as 11–18 schools was approved in 1967.

Bath

A plan covering county and Church of England voluntary schools for five 11–18 single sex schools was approved in October 1969.

Bedfordshire

A plan based on 9–13 middle schools covering county and voluntary schools was approved in May 1968. Implementation in some areas is due to begin in 1971.

Berkshire

Plans for the whole of the County covering county and voluntary Church of England and non-denominational schools, have been approved mainly on the basis of 11–18 schools.

Bexley

A plan (which replaces one approved in May 1967 and subsequently withdrawn) covering both county and Roman Catholic voluntary schools is under consideration by the Department.

Birkenhead

A plan based on 8–12 middle schools and 12–18 comprehensive schools was approved for county and Church of England voluntary schools in 1968, and will begin to be implemented in September 1970. A similar scheme for Roman Catholic voluntary aided schools was approved in December 1969. This provides for 12–16 comprehensive schools, a sixth form centre for girls and provision for sixth form boys in a direct grant school.

Birmingham

A plan for county schools only was rejected in September 1968 because it retained nearly all the existing grammar schools. The authority have a number of comprehensive schools which compete with grammar schools for the most able pupils through selection tests at 11+.

Blackburn

Short and long term plans for county and Church of England schools were approved in August 1966. An interim 11–16/14–18 plan with optional transfer at 14 was implemented in September 1966 and changed to an 11–16 and 11–18 pattern in September 1968. All schools will be 11–18 in the long term.

A short term Roman Catholic scheme with 11–16

schools and optional transfer at 14+ to the two single-sex direct grant schools was introduced in September 1967.

Blackpool

A plan for county schools was approved in 1966. It envisages 11–16 and 11–18 comprehensive schools. A direct grant school and an independent school will be involved to the extent of accepting local education authority pupils of a broader range of ability than at present.

Bolton

The authority have declined to submit a scheme which eliminates selection.

Bootle

Proposals were submitted to the Secretary of State in November 1969 and are under consideration.

Bournemouth

The authority have declined to submit a scheme.

Bradford

An interim scheme covering county schools was put into operation in 1964, comprising 11–13 and 13–16 and 13–18 schools and it was revised in September 1968 to comprise 11–13 and 13–18 schools only. The authority have decided that the next phase shall incorporate 9–13 middle schools and are discussing a scheme for one fifth of the city which is unlikely to be capable of implementation before 1971; the remaining areas of the city should be reorganised on a self-contained basis over the following decade. The authority already operate a purpose-built middle school.

Breconshire

All maintained schools are organised on comprehensive lines except in the Brecon and Gwerynfed areas.

Brent

Brent introduced comprehensive education in September 1967. The long term plan covering both county and Roman Catholic voluntary aided schools based on all through 11–18 schools should be implemented by about 1972.

Brighton

Interim proposals, submitted in 1967, will be considered by the Department when an indication of long-term proposals is received.

Bristol

Reorganised in most areas since 1965 on a pattern of either 11–18 all through schools or 11–15/13–18 schools with transfer at 13 for academic pupils on the basis of guided parental choice, and covering both county and voluntary schools.

Bromley

A plan based on 11–18 schools, covering both county and Roman Catholic voluntary schools was approved in March 1968.

Buckinghamshire

The authority have not submitted any formal plan for reorganisation.

Burnley

An interim plan for county schools and a voluntary controlled school was approved in 1966 and has been implemented. It is based on 11–16 and 13–18 schools with transfer by parental option at 13. In addition there are two 11–18 comprehensive schools, one county and one Roman Catholic voluntary aided.

Burton on Trent

A plan covering all county and voluntary schools, based on

11–16 and 11–18 comprehensive schools, was approved in 1969. It is expected to come into operation in 1973.

Bury

The authority have declined to submit a scheme. They are building one county comprehensive school in the Unsworth area.

Canterbury

A plan for 9–13 middle schools was approved in May 1969 for County and Church of England voluntary schools.

Caernarvonshire

The majority of the county is already reorganised. The remaining area, Bangor and Pwllheli, will be reorganised from September 1971 on completion of approved building projects.

Cambridgeshire

Plans for the Wisbech and March areas were approved in August 1967. Long-term plans are for a system of 11–16 and 11–18 schools. Plans for the remainder of Cambridgeshire are being discussed.

Cardiff

An interim scheme introduced in September 1965 provided for 11–16 schools with optional transfer at 13+ to 13–18 schools. A long-term scheme based on 11–18 and 11–16 schools was approved in August 1969.

Cardiganshire

All areas are reorganised except Aberystwyth and Llandyssul.

Carlisle

A plan for 11–16 and 11–18 schools was implemented in 1968.

Carmarthenshire

All-through 11–18 schools are already agreed for Llandovery, Amman Valley and Llandeilo. Plans for other areas have still to be submitted.

Cheshire

Cheshire's plans are prepared on a divisional basis. So far the following seven divisional areas have had plans approved: Bebington, East Cheshire, Hyde and Longdendale, Crewe, SE Cheshire (Alsager only), Ellesmere Port (Stanney schools only) and Knutsford. Plans for a further five areas are under consideration by the Department: Sale and Lymm, Dukinfield and Stalybridge, Mid-Cheshire (Winsford and Tarporley only), Deeside (Neston only) and Tarvin. All the plans so far submitted are either for 11–18 schools or for 11–16 schools with sixth form college.

Chester

A scheme based on 8–12 middle schools with 12–18 comprehensive schools for both county and voluntary schools was approved in June 1969, and is planned to start in 1972.

Cornwall

Plans for most of the County are already approved. Patterns vary from area to area and include 11–16 schools with sixth form college, two tier 11–14 and 14–18 schools, and 11–16 and 11–18 schools.

Coventry

The authority have been developing purpose-built comprehensive schools over the last 20 years and were over two-thirds reorganised before Circular 10/65 on the basis of 11–18 schools. A Roman Catholic scheme for two 11–18 comprehensive schools was approved in January 1969.

Croydon

A plan for a mixture of 11–16 and two tier 11–14, 14–18 schools was approved in September 1968. It is due to be implemented by 1971.

Cumberland

A plan approved in April 1967, but excluding Keswick, comprises 11–18 comprehensive schools, 10–13 middle schools, and in four areas, Whitehaven, Workington, Cockermouth and Penrith, an 11–16/13–18 system involving guided parental choice at the age of 13.

Darlington

A plan was approved in August 1965, providing for 11–16 schools with sixth form college. Implementation has begun. A Roman Catholic scheme providing an 11–18 school was approved in May 1967.

Denbighshire

The interim pattern for all areas was introduced in September 1967 involving a mixture of 11–18 schools, two tier schools and 11–16 schools with sixth form college.

Derby

A revised County and Roman Catholic plan for all through schools is under consideration by the Department.

Derbyshire

One-third of the County was reorganised by 1969. The pattern adopted varies from area to area. There are 11–16 and 11–18 schools, 11–15/14–18 schools (with transfer at 14 by parental choice) and two tier 11–14, 14–18 schools. Three area schemes are under consideration by the Department.

Devon

Five comprehensive schools were in operation or approved

prior to the authority's main submission. A scheme was approved for most of the County in December 1966 based mainly on 11–16/11–18 and 11–14/14–18 patterns. Proposals for Barnstaple were approved in October 1969 for 11–16 schools with sixth form college incorporated in the North Devon Technical College.

Dewsbury

A plan for 8–12 middle schools and sixth form college was approved in 1967 for county schools. Implementation will probably take place in 1972.

Doncaster

A long term 9–13 middle school plan was approved in 1968. An interim 11–16/13–18 plan, with transfer at 13 by parental option, was introduced in the same year.

Dorset

Four areas were already served by comprehensive schools in 1964. Plans for other parts of the county approved so far are for 9–13 middle schools, two tier 11–14, 14–18 schools and (in Poole Excepted District) 8–12 middle schools and sixth form college.

Dudley

A long term 11–18 plan for county and voluntary schools was approved in April 1968, but the authority were asked to reconsider their short term proposals. A revised plan for 8–12 middle schools and three sixth form colleges was received November 1969 and is now under consideration. These proposals include a 12–18 Roman Catholic comprehensive school.

Durham

A plan for 11–18 schools covering county and voluntary schools was approved in 1969 and implementation has begun.

Ealing

In 1966 the authority reorganised the schools in Acton into three 11–18 all through comprehensive schools and also produced an acceptable plan for Southall, to be implemented in 1968. Two unsatisfactory plans for Ealing were rejected in December 1966 and February 1968. Subsequently the proposals for Southall were withdrawn. Fresh proposals are under consideration by the authority but have not yet been submitted to the Department.

Eastbourne

A long term plan for 11–16 schools with a sixth form college was approved in August 1967.

Enfield

A plan for county and voluntary schools was fully implemented by January 1968 and is based on two tier 11–14, 14–18 schools.

Essex

Most divisions of the County have now had plans approved, mainly for 11–18 schools. The plans for two areas, Thurrock and South East Essex, are for 11–16 schools with sixth form colleges.

Exeter

A plan was approved in August 1969, for 5–8/8–12/12–16 schools and a combined sixth form and Further Education College, based on the existing Exeter College of Further Education.

Flintshire

An interim plan for a mixture of 11–18 and 11–13, 13–18 schools was implemented in 1967. The long term pattern is 11–18 schools in all areas.

Gateshead

A plan for County schools was implemented in 1968 when a two tier 11–14, 14–18 pattern was introduced. Approval of

a scheme to reorganise one of the Roman Catholic
secondary schools, as an 11–18 comprehensive school
followed in May 1969. A proposal for an 11–14, 14–18
Roman Catholic school is being reconsidered.

Glamorgan

The final proposals for the County have not yet been
received but draft proposals show an ultimate pattern of all
through schools. Interim arrangements are mixed but are
generally of a two tier pattern. Areas now reorganised are
Kenfig and Port Talbot Division, Maesteg, Mountain Ash,
Garw, Barry (Boys only) and Swansea Valley (Pontardawe
area), all based on 11–18 schools.

Gloucester

The authority's plan was rejected in July 1967 because it
retained selection. A revised scheme is awaited.

Gloucestershire

Plans have been approved for all but four areas of the
county, generally of an 11–16/11–18 pattern. One third of
secondary school pupils should be in comprehensive
schools by September 1970.

Great Yarmouth

A scheme based on 9–13 middle schools was approved in
1968.

Grimsby

A plan for 8–12 middle schools and 12–18 upper schools
was approved in February 1967. Roman Catholic schools
are included in this scheme.

Halifax

A scheme proposing a system of 8–12 middle schools was
submitted in 1967, but it is being reconsidered by the
authority. Approval was given in October 1969 to the
reorganisation of a Roman Catholic Secondary school as
an 11–18 comprehensive school.

Hampshire

Plans for the greater part of the County have already been approved based on all through 11–18 schools or 11–16 schools with sixth form colleges. Schemes in two areas have already been implemented and more will follow during the 1970s. Proposals for the Winchester area are now under consideration by the Department.

Haringey

A plan for 11–18 schools was approved in January 1967 and implemented in September of that year. The Roman Catholic schools in the Borough are also reorganised on a two tier basis.

Harrow

Harrow have produced two unacceptable plans, rejected in January 1967 and October 1968. Both plans perpetuated a collegiate system involving the association of grammar and secondary modern schools and a change in the age of transfer to 12. A revised scheme is awaited.

Hartlepool

A plan for 11–18 schools was approved in October 1968, with an amending interim proposal in May 1969 allowing for some 11–16 schools in the short term. Implementation should take place in 1971.

Hastings

A plan for 8–12 middle schools was approved in October 1968.

Havering

A plan for 11–18 schools was approved in August 1967. The authority are now working towards an implementation date of 1972/73. Discussions on the reorganisation of Roman Catholic schools are proceeding.

Herefordshire

A plan was approved in 1967. It provides for 11–16 and

11–18 schools in most areas, 11–16 schools with sixth form college in Hereford, and a 9–13 middle school in Ledbury.

Hertfordshire

Plans for all but two areas have been approved. The approved schemes include a number of 11–18 schools, and 9–13 middle schools in two areas.

Hillingdon

An 8–12 middle school plan was rejected in March 1967. Revised proposals have not yet been submitted to the Department.

Hounslow

A plan for all through schools (with one two tier arrangement) was approved in November 1967 and largely implemented.

Huddersfield

A plan for 11–16 schools with sixth form colleges was approved in 1967.

Huntingdon and Peterborough

Plans covering county and denominational voluntary schools have been approved. They provide 11–16 and 11–18 comprehensive schools with some two tier 11–14, 14–18 arrangements. Reorganisation is expected to be completed during the early 1970s.

Inner London

A plan (the second—the first having been withdrawn) was submitted in February 1968, and approved in principle in July of that year. The plan, which covers all maintained and voluntary aided schools is limited to the period up to 1975. It provides for a reduction in the number of grammar schools from 68 to 44 and an increase in the number of comprehensive schools from 81 to 128. By 1975 the number of modern schools will be reduced to 27.

Ipswich

A plan for 11–16 schools (the 16–19 arrangements were not defined) was submitted in 1966. The Authority were asked to reconsider their proposals in 1968 and a revised scheme is awaited.

Isles of Scilly

A 11–16 school with sixth form college provision on the mainland has been operated since 1967.

Isle of Wight

A long term plan to introduce a 9–13 middle school pattern, with interim proposals for 11–13 and 13–18 schools, was approved in 1967. The interim scheme will come into operation in 1971.

Kent

Plans including a number of different patterns of reorganisation have been approved for all but two divisions of Kent. In some areas the authority are already operating two tier 11–16/13–18 schemes with parental option to transfer at 13. Some 9–13 middle school proposals are to be implemented area by area, beginning in September 1970.

Kingston-upon-Hull

A 9–13 middle school plan for county schools was approved in 1966 and revised proposals on a similar pattern for Roman Catholic schools were approved in 1968. Both schemes came into operation in September 1969.

Kingston-upon-Thames

The authority's plan was rejected in December 1966 because it retained selection. The authority have not produced an alternative plan.

Lancashire

Long and short term plans for County and Church of England voluntary schools have been approved for 16 of the 29 divisions of the County, and for Roman Catholic schools in 2 divisions. Long term schemes have been approved in a further eight divisions. The usual pattern is 11–18 schools but there will be 11–16 schools with sixth form colleges in eight divisions, and 9–13 middle schools in a small part of one division. In the short term there will be some 11–16 schools combined with 11–18 schools and some two tier 11–14, 14–18 and 11–16, 13–18 schools. Implementation began in 1967. In three divisions county and Church of England schools and in two divisions Roman Catholic schools, were completely reorganised by 1969, with others partially, and implementation continuing on a school by school basis.

Leeds

The authority's original plan was withdrawn but a new submission has just been received. It follows a 9–13 middle school pattern.

Leicester

A long term plan for 11–16 comprehensive schools with sixth form colleges was approved in April 1969.

Leicestershire

Reorganisation began in 1957 on the basis of two tier 11–15/14–18 schools with transfer to the upper schools by parental choice. The county was reorganised on this basis, with some 11–18 comprehensive schools, by September 1969. The authority plan to move in 1972 to a long term plan based on 11–14 and 14–18 schools with automatic transfer at 14 and some 11–18 schools. Voluntary schools are included.

Lincoln

An 8–12 middle school scheme was approved in July 1968

for implementation in 1972; the Roman Catholic schools were included.

Lincolnshire Holland

A long term 9–13 middle school scheme was approved in January 1967.

Lincolnshire Kesteven

A scheme for the Lincoln fringe area was approved in November 1968 to be implemented in September 1970. There will be three 11–18 schools, two at North Hykeham and one at Branston. Plans for other parts of the County are under consideration by the authority.

Lincolnshire Lindsey

A plan covering all the authority's area, save Scunthorpe Excepted District, Louth and South East Lindsey, was approved in August 1967. It is based on a mixture of 11–16 schools, all through 11–18, and two tier 11–14, 14–18 schools. A scheme for Scunthorpe Excepted District providing for 11–16 schools and a sixth form college was approved in June 1967, implementation beginning in September 1968. An interim two tier 11–14, 14–18 scheme was approved for Louth before the issue of Circular 10/65 and is already implemented.

Liverpool

The Authority began to develop 11–18 county comprehensive schools before Circular 10/65. A plan designed to complete the process was withdrawn by the Authority in 1967.

Luton

A plan for county schools based on 11–16 comprehensives with a sixth form college has been in operation since 1966. A proposal for an 11–18 Roman Catholic school has been approved.

Manchester

A plan covering county schools based on an 11–18 system was approved in 1966 and implemented in 1967.

Merioneth

All maintained schools are already reorganised on comprehensive lines.

Merthyr Tydfil

The approved interim and long-term pattern is for three all through 11–18 schools, and includes a Roman Catholic school.

Merton

A plan for 9–13 middle schools covering county and voluntary schools was implemented in September 1969.

Monmouthshire

Schemes have been accepted for most parts of the county involving a mixture of all through 11–18 and two tier 11–14, 14–18 schools. Most areas will be reorganised by 1972.

Montgomeryshire

Already organised on comprehensive lines.

Newcastle upon Tyne

An 11–18 all through system was introduced in the western area of the city in 1965 and in the eastern area in 1967.

Newham

A revised plan for 11–18 all through schools which envisages implementation in 1972 was approved in August 1969. Plans for the reorganisation of Roman Catholic schools are under discussion.

Newport

Both interim and long term plans were approved in 1966. The long term pattern is for all through 11–18 schools. The interim pattern, which was introduced in September 1966, covers both all through schools and two tier schools with automatic transfer at 13.

Norfolk

The authority have informed the Department that they intend to achieve a comprehensive system of education. Formal, detailed proposals have not yet been submitted.

Northampton

A plan approved in 1968 provides in the short term for 11–16/13–18 schools, with transfer by parental choice at 13, developing in the long term to a 9–13 middle school pattern. Implementation begins in 1970. A Roman Catholic long term plan is under consideration.

Northamptonshire

Plans for most of the county have been approved and the authority have given a declaration of intent to reorganise the remaining six areas on all through lines when population growth makes this possible.

A mixed pattern is proposed in the short term with some all through 11–18 schools and some two tier arrangements. The long term pattern will comprise 11–18 schools and 9–13 middle schools. Implementation has started in some areas.

Northumberland

A 9–13 middle school scheme was approved in January 1968, for implementation area by area from 1969 onwards.

Norwich

An 8–12 middle school scheme was approved in 1967, and will come into operation in September 1970.

Nottingham

The authority's plan proposed 11–16 schools and one experimental college covering the 16–19 age group. The authority were asked in 1969 to reconsider their proposals for the 16–19 age group.

Nottinghamshire

Approval was given in 1967 to a scheme covering county and Church of England voluntary schools. In different parts of the county there will be 11–16 and 11–18 schools leading to sixth form colleges and some two tier 11–13, 13–16/18 schools.

Oldham

A scheme based on 11–16 and 11–18 comprehensive schools began in 1966. Reorganisation of Roman Catholic schools followed in 1967 and established 11–16 comprehensives with sixth form provision in Manchester direct grant schools.

Oxford

A 9–13 middle school scheme was approved for County and Roman Catholic schools in January 1968 and January 1969 respectively. Proposals for Church of England voluntary schools have not yet been submitted.

Oxfordshire

The County was partly reorganised prior to Circular 10/65 and plans for the remainder, involving a mixed pattern of 11–16 and 11–18 schools and 11–14 and 14–18 schools and covering county and Church of England schools were approved in August 1967. In two areas there are 11–16/ 13–18 interim arrangements, with transfer by guided parental choice at 13.

Pembrokeshire

Some areas are already reorganised on comprehensive lines.

A scheme for the Pembroke-Pembroke Dock area was approved in August 1969 but proposals for the remaining areas are awaited.

Plymouth

A plan was rejected in December 1969 and a revised scheme is awaited. The authority already operates two comprehensive schools.

Portsmouth

An 8–12 middle school scheme covering county and voluntary schools was approved in June 1969.

Preston

A plan covering County and Church of England voluntary schools, based on 11–16 comprehensive schools with sixth form college, was approved and put into operation in 1967. Maintained Roman Catholic secondary schools have operated since 1967 as 11–16 schools admitting pupils on a comprehensive basis with pupils attending Catholic direct grant schools for sixth form work.

Radnorshire

The County will be served by two comprehensive schools—one at Presteigne and the other at Llandrindod Wells, beginning in 1970 and 1971 respectively.

Reading

A revised plan for 11–18 schools was submitted in December 1969 and is under consideration by the Department.

Redbridge

A plan was approved in principle in November 1968 and proposed 11–18 schools to be developed over a period of years. The authority are reconsidering their proposal for a sixth form college in one part of the Borough. Proposals for the Roman Catholic voluntary aided and direct grant schools are still under discussion.

Richmond upon Thames

The authority's plan was rejected in December 1966 because it retained selection. The authority have not produced an alternative plan.

Rochdale

A short term plan for county and voluntary schools, with transfers at 14 by parental option from 11–16 schools to 14–18 schools, has been in operation since 1965. Long term proposals, with a fully comprehensive pattern based on 10–13 middle schools, were approved in 1969. County and Church of England schools will adopt the middle school pattern in 1970, Roman Catholic schools in 1975.

Rotherham

A plan for 11–16 schools with sixth form college was implemented in 1966.

Rutland

The authority have declined to submit a plan.

St Helens

Long and short term plans for both County and voluntary schools have been approved. The interim scheme is for 11–16 schools with transfer at 13 by guided parental choice to 13–18 schools. (For Roman Catholics the option is to transfer to direct grant schools). The interim proposals, which have been implemented, will eventually give way to a scheme for all through 11–18 schools.

Salford

The authority have not so far submitted a scheme.

Sheffield

The scheme approved in November 1968 provided for a long-term pattern of 8–12, 12–16/12–18 schools. Implementation began in September 1969 and will be phased over a period of years. The Roman Catholics ended selection in September 1969, when three schools became 11–16 comprehensive schools with transfer on parental option at 13 or 16 to two direct grant schools. A long term scheme is under consideration.

Salop

Plans already approved for part of the County provide for 11–16 and 11–18 schools in eight areas and 9–13 middle schools in one area. A scheme for Shrewsbury was rejected in May 1968 because it proposed the retention of grammar schools.

Solihull

A scheme providing for all through 11–18 schools was approved in 1967. This includes a Roman Catholic voluntary school. Implementation is expected to begin in 1972.

Somerset

Plans are already approved for the major part of the County and provide for a variety of patterns including 11–16 and 11–18 schools, 9–13 middle schools and 11–18 all through schools. Proposals for a further four areas in the County are under consideration by the Department.

South Shields

A long term plan for 11–18 schools was approved in 1967. At the same time an interim scheme proposing all through schools in split premises was rejected. The authority are still considering an interim scheme.

Southampton

A revised plan was approved in May 1968 covering county and Roman Catholic voluntary schools providing for 8–12 middle schools, leading either to 12–18 schools or to 12–16 schools and sixth form colleges.

Southend on Sea

A plan submitted by the authority was rejected and a revised scheme has not yet been received by the Department.

Southport

In 1968 the authority submitted a short term 11–16/13–18 scheme with transfer at 13 by guided parental choice, and were asked to submit a long term plan. This has not yet been received. A plan for one 11–18 all through Roman Catholic comprehensive school was approved in July 1968, to be implemented in 1970.

Staffordshire

Proposals for 11–18 county comprehensive schools serving a number of the areas in the County were approved in 1968. Some comprehensive schools have already been established; others will come into operation when additional buildings are provided. Similar proposals for Roman Catholic schools have been approved in principle. Schemes for the remaining areas have not yet been submitted to the Department.

Stockport

The authority withdrew their original proposals in 1969 and have informed the Department that they intend to reorganise on the basis of a middle school pattern.

Stoke on Trent

An 8–12 middle school system with a sixth form college, was approved in 1967 and selection will end in 1970. An

8–12 middle school scheme for Roman Catholic schools was approved in November 1969, and will also come into operation in 1970. In the Roman Catholic scheme, pupils will transfer at 12 without selection either to high schools or direct grant schools. The latter will cater for all sixth formers.

Suffolk East

A plan based on 9–13 middle schools has been approved in principle for the whole of the County (except Felixstowe which has been reorganised on a two tier 11–14, 14–18 basis since 1966) and will begin in some areas in 1971.

Suffolk West

A plan based on 9–13 middle schools was approved in 1967.

Sunderland

A plan was approved in March 1967 for 11–18 all through schools. The first comprehensive school opened in September 1966. A Roman Catholic long term scheme of one 11–16 and three 11–18 schools was included in the approval.

Surrey

A scheme which retained selection was rejected in 1967. Following this the authority resolved to reorganise two areas by 1971 and to proceed as and when possible to the elimination of selection in other areas. Middle school schemes (9–13 and 8–12) for some parts of the County were approved in July 1968 and July 1969. Similar proposals for Roman Catholic schools in most areas have also been approved.

Sussex East

Plans covering the county schools were approved in August 1967, based on an 11–16 and 11–18 system.

Sussex West

Five comprehensive schools were in existence prior to the

submission of plans. The plans, providing a pattern of 11–16 and 11–18 schools, and in one area, 10–13 middle schools, were approved in March 1969. Plans for two areas are at present being considered.

Sutton

The authority produced a plan in December 1966 which was rejected in April 1967 because it retained selection. Revised proposals have not yet been submitted.

Swansea

The long term pattern is for all through 11–18 schools. The interim pattern, which the authority hope to introduce in September 1970, includes some two tier schools.

Teeside

Part of the authority, Middlesborough, was reorganised in 1966 on the basis of 11–16/13–18 schools with transfer by parental option at 13. This scheme included Roman Catholic schools. Proposals for the rest of the area and a long term plan for Middlesborough are awaited.

Torbay

No plan has yet been submitted.

Tynemouth

A plan was approved in August 1966, for implementation in September 1969. Until a sixth form college is built there will be some 11–18 schools as well as 11–16 schools.

Wakefield

Selection at 11+ was abolished in September 1965, when the authority began to operate an interim scheme involving transfer by parental choice at 13+. They have recently been discussing an 11–13, 13–18 scheme with automatic transfer at 13 and are seeking ultimately to have a 9–13 middle school system.

Wallasey

A plan for 9–13 middle schools was approved for county schools in June 1967 and similar proposals for Roman Catholic voluntary aided schools in May 1968. Transitional arrangements for the implementation of these schemes began in 1967 and 1968 respectively.

Walsall

A long term plan was submitted in January 1969 for 11–18 comprehensive schools. A short term scheme is awaited.

Waltham Forest

A plan, based on a two tier pattern 11–14 and 14–18 was approved in April 1967 and implemented in September 1968. Proposals for Roman Catholic schools are under discussion.

Warley

No plan has yet been submitted.

Warrington

A plan covering both county and voluntary schools is under consideration by the Department.

Warwickshire

A plan for 11–18 schools was approved in 1967. Revised proposals for an 8–12 middle school scheme and a sixth form college in one area (Nuneaton Excepted District), were approved in September 1969. Proposals for South Warwickshire are awaited. The Chelmsley Wood overspill area is to reorganise in 1971.

West Bromwich

A plan for 11–16 and 11–18 schools was approved in 1968 and implemented in 1969. Roman Catholic schools were included in the approved scheme.

Westmorland

The authority have declined to submit a plan but already operate three comprehensive schools.

Wigan

A plan for county and Church of England schools is based on 10–13 middle schools and was approved in August 1969. A start is planned in 1972.

Wiltshire

Reorganisation is being planned on an area by area basis. The general pattern is for all through 11–18 schools.

Wolverhampton

The authority's plan for 11–18 schools, county and voluntary, was rejected in 1968 because no proposals were made for Wolverhampton Boys Grammar (non-denominational voluntary aided) and the Girls' High School. Although selection for these schools is continuing, a number of comprehensive schools are in operation.

Worcester

The authority have declined to submit a plan.

Worcestershire

A plan for 9–13 middle schools, county and voluntary Church of England, in most of the county and 8–12 middle schools in three areas was approved in 1968. Plans for three small areas are awaited.

York

A 9–13 middle school scheme was approved in March 1967. It did not include Roman Catholic schools.

Yorkshire East Riding

A plan for 11–16 and 11–18 schools was approved in principle in June 1967. In one area a 9–13 middle school feeds into an 11–18 school. Reorganisation is being implemented in stages, the first comprehensive school having been set up in 1962.

Yorkshire North Riding

A plan approved in July 1969, is based on two tier and all through schools and in two places, Scarborough and Guisborough, 11–16 schools with sixth form colleges. Implementation will be by stages but the scheme is expected to be largely implemented between 1970 and 1972.

Yorkshire West Riding

This area comprises 20 Divisional Executives, seven County Districts and the Keighley Excepted District. Schemes for most of the Divisions were approved in December 1966 and include middle schools, 11–18 schools, and 11–16 schools with sixth form centres attached to 11–18 schools. Reorganisation is being implemented on a piecemeal basis over a long term but to date there are 18 middle schools and 38 comprehensive schools. In general, Church of England schools are being integrated with divisional reorganisation schemes and the Roman Catholic authorities have established comprehensive schools in some areas. Keighley Excepted District reorganised in September 1967 with a two tier interim arrangement involving parental option at 14, but from September 1969 parental option ended. The long term intention here is for a 10–13 middle school system.

Printed in England for Her Majesty's Stationery Office
by James Townsend and Sons Ltd. Dd. 153861 K 320 2/70.